A Practical Guide to Funeral Rites In Islam

(2nd Edition)

Maulana Ebrahim Noor

Islamic Academy of Coventry

Islamic Academy of Coventry
Funeral Rites in Islām

1st Edition – 2015

2nd Edition - 2019

For abba - Ḥāji Kasim Kathrada

CONTENTS

FOREWORD

In the name of Allāh ﷻ, the Beneficent, the Merciful. All praise belongs to Allāh ﷻ, the Lord of the universe and Master of our fortunes. Peace and blessings upon the best of creation who illuminated the world, and upon his companions and all those who follow in his footsteps until the day of judgement.

Islām is a complete religion that provides guidance regarding all matters of life including for moments of happiness and grief. This guidance is underpinned with simplicity and a focus on following the Prophetic Sunnah. It is a sad fact that we have imposed certain cultural practices and innovations upon ourselves and complicated matters that were devised simple and easy. The way in which we conduct ourselves during marriages and deaths illustrate this. My respected father, Shaykhul Ḥadīth Mufti Shabbir Ahmed Sahib mentions that even dying has become an expensive matter. By the grace of Almighty Allāh ﷻ, my respected colleague Mawlānā Ebrahim Noor Sahib has compiled this book trying to address this, by detailing the Prophetic Sunnah and guidance regarding the deceased. The book dispels many myths and is supplemented with references from the books of Ḥadīth and jurisprudence.

Upon the death of a family member, most families in the UK struggle with understanding and managing the end to end process of burial. This book is unique in this regard as it provides a step by step guide for the end to end process in light of the legal framework of England. Thus, this book is extremely beneficial for Muslims across the UK. Whilst some aspects of the process are unique to Coventry, the book can be adapted by other towns and cities as most of the processes are the same.

I pray to Almighty Allāh ﷻ to make this book beneficial and a means of guidance and grant us a good death in the state of faith.

Yusuf Shabbir,

Blackburn, UK

1 Dhul Qaʿdah 1436 H.

www.islamicportal.co.uk

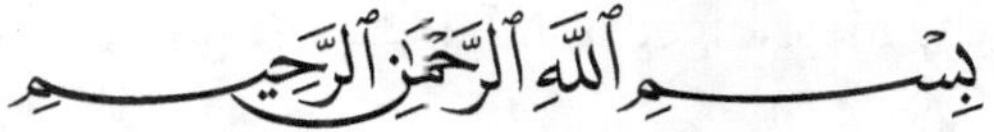

INTRODUCTION

All Praise is to Allāh ﷾ the Lord of the Worlds, Master of the Creation, the Forgiving, and the Merciful. Birth, life and death, this is the circle of life. A person is born into this world, spends a little time and then passes away. Allāh ﷾ mentions in the Holy Qur'ān:

$$كُلُّ نَفْسٍ ذَآئِقَةُ الْمَوْتِ^{1}$$

"Every soul has to taste death"

The one thing we can all be sure about and cannot deny, is the fact that one day we will all be leaving this earth. Our life on this earth is merely a journey to our real abode in the hereafter. The Messenger of Allāh ﷺ mentions in a Ḥadīth:

$$كُنْ فِي الدُّنْيَا كَأَنَّكَ غَرِيبٌ أَوْ عَابِرُ سَبِيلٍ^{2}$$

"Live in this world as if you are a traveller or a wayfarer".

---

[1] Sūrah Āl-ʿImrān verse 185

[2] Jāmiʿ al-Tirmidhī 2255

In another Ḥadīth, the Messenger of Allāh ﷺ mentions:

الْكَيِّسُ مَنْ دَانَ نَفْسَهُ وَعَمِلَ لِمَا بَعْدَ الْمَوْتِ وَالْعَاجِزُ مَنْ أَتْبَعَ نَفْسَهُ هَوَاهَا وَتَمَنَّى عَلَى اللَّهِ³

"The intelligent person is the one who controls his self-desires and performs deeds for after his death, and the helpless person is the one who follows his self-desires and relies on Allāh سُبْحَانَهُوَتَعَالَى"

This booklet does not go over all the preparations one must make before they pass away as our whole lives should be preparation for the hereafter, but I will cover the necessary steps we must take as Muslims when another Muslim is about to pass away or passes away.

This is a time of great grief and sadness which can lead people to perform acts which are against Sharī‘ah and are classified as 'Bid‘ah' - innovation. People sometimes spend lavishly on funerals in the same way as they spend at weddings. People become a burden on the family of the deceased expecting to be dined on several occasions and the atmosphere at the funeral house may become contrary to the event. Many actions are done with the thinking that there is a basis for it in our religion, but the reality is that there is no evidence to support them.

---

[3] Jāmi‘ al-Tirmidhī 2383

Rather than go through all the innovative practises, I have identified the actions for which there is sound evidence. I have provided references where required, so we can have peace of mind that we are carrying out all of the rituals correctly. We will comprehensively review the process which will enable the burial to take place quickly, easily and most importantly in accordance with Sharīʿah.

Some of the subjects we will cover are as follows:

- What do we do when we see someone passing away?
- What legal paperwork do we need to go through with the burial?
- How to prepare the Kafan (shroud) and bathe the body of the deceased
- The correct burial process according to Sharīʿah
- The period of mourning and information on ʿIddah
- Etiquettes of visiting the house of the deceased
- What can we do for those who have passed away?

Another major factor we must address is that each town/city has different burial arrangements with their local councils. This could be regarding the times of burials, all the way through to whether the burial has to take place within a coffin/casket or not.

For reference, I have extensively used various texts including compilations on Ḥadīth & Fiqh, all of which are referenced throughout the booklet: I have also used the booklet "What to do when a Muslim Dies" which is available on www.islamicbulletin.org. May Allāh سُبْحَانَهُوَتَعَالَ grant the compilers of all these resources and all other resources, success in both worlds.

Since the release of the initial edition in 2015, I have been wanting to update the booklet, but due to other commitments, I have been unable to do so. It was only upon the demise of my dear father in law early last year, whilst referencing the booklet myself and speaking to my dear teachers Mufti Shabbir Saheb and Maulānā Abdul Raheem Saheb that I identified many areas where the booklet could be improved. Also seeing the efficiency of the local Funeral Committee in Gloucester & how the Hospital were very receptive to our requirements as Muslims, made me want to include some advice on these subjects as well.

Furthermore, Maulānā Yusuf Shabbir has released some excellent articles on islamicportal.co.uk relating to Funeral Rites. I have decided to include this information on these important aspects within this edition.

In the Appendices, I have included 3 very important documents.

- A Statutory Declaration for those Muslims who feel there may be a risk after their demise of not getting an Islamic Burial.
- An Islamic Will Template (based on the 1st Ethical Will Template). Each adult Muslim should have prepared an Islamic Will.
- Testator's Asset & Finance Identifier. Another essential document which needs to be filled in and kept with the Islamic Will, so your executors/family will be able to identify all your Assets and household finances which you currently manage.

The above documents can be filled in and removed from the booklet if necessary.

I would like thanks all of the Scholars, friends and members of Funeral Committees who have helped me in preparing and verifying this booklet.

Special mention for the following:

- Mufti Ebrahim Desai Ḥafiẓahullāh who gave me permission to include his excellent & comprehensive article on ʿIddah
- Shaykh Yunus Dudhwala Ḥafiẓahullāh who helped me compile the section 'Advice for Chaplains'
- Maulānā Yusuf Shabbir Ḥafiẓahullāh whose work I have included in this edition and is always available to answer many of my queries, not just on this subject but on many others as well
- Ismail Mehter (Bereavement Administrator for the Muslim Burial Council of Gloucester) who helped compile the section 'Advice for Burial Committees'

May Allāh سُبْحَانَهُوَتَعَالَى make them all a means of guidance for the Ummah and grant them success in both worlds.

Finally, by going through this material, it will Inshā'Allāh remind us all of our final abode. I pray that Allāh سُبْحَانَهُوَتَعَالَى grants us all the ability to follow the Sunnah of Rasūlullāh صَلَّىٱللَّهُعَلَيْهِوَسَلَّم, to stay away from innovation, prepare correctly before our final journey and help other prepare as well.

Āmīn.

Ebrahim Noor 17ᵗʰ Safar 1441 AH (17ᵗʰ October 2019 - 2ⁿᵈ Edition)

PREPARING A WILL

A person cannot be sure of the time or place when they are going to pass away. As a Muslim, it is our duty to fulfil the rights of other people, which they have over us. One of these main rights is the right of inheritance which leads to the preparation of a Will.

عَنِ ابْنِ عُمَرَ أَنَّ رَسُولَ اللَّهِ صلى الله عليه وسلم قَالَ

" مَا حَقُّ امْرِئٍ مُسْلِمٍ لَهُ شَىْءٌ يُرِيدُ أَنْ يُوصِىَ فِيهِ يَبِيتُ لَيْلَتَيْنِ إِلاَّ وَوَصِيَّتُهُ مَكْتُوبَةٌ عِنْدَهُ " [4]

Ibn ʿUmar ﷺ narrates that Rasūlullāh ﷺ said "It is the duty of a Muslim who has something which is to be given as a bequest not to have it for two nights without having his Will written down regarding it"

The Holy Qurʾān mentions in detail the proportion of a person's wealth which must go to the respective relation. There are also many Aḥādīth which also state the importance of preparing our Wills. Theoretically, if our wealth was easily identifiable and we lived in a country where it would automatically be distributed according to Islamic law, then we could be fairly confident that our estate would be divided correctly. However, the truth of the matter is that many of us have wealth which is not common knowledge, for example we

---

[4] Ṣaḥīḥ Muslim 1627

might have multiple properties, different bank accounts, shared accounts and properties in different countries as well.

As well as having our own assets, many people nowadays also have mortgages, loans from banks, loans from people which are not common knowledge. Many people give money as Qarḍ-e-Ḥasanah (interest free loan for a good cause) as well. So you can see how important it is to identify what a person actually owns and what they owe, to establish the value of a person's estate.

Here are a few points to consider.

- If you do not leave a Will behind, the inheritance laws of this land will not distribute your wealth according to Islamic Law
- Not leaving a Will can lead to internal family disputes during the distribution of wealth
- Islām has set fixed proportions of a person's wealth for certain relatives after they pass away
- You can use up to one third of your wealth of your estate to distribute as you wish
- The rest of your wealth from the estate will be divided according to Islamic Law
- You cannot make a bequest for anyone who will inherit from you.

So what do we need to do next?

- Work out the total value of your estate, which includes, properties, cash, gold, all assets however minute that are under sole ownership.
- Work out the amount of money or assets you owe to third parties which includes, loans, mortgages etc.

- Calculate the proportion owned in shared accounts, properties and assets.

- Identify any assets which have been borrowed or belong to another person.

- Identify any parties you would like to contribute to, from one third of your estate and how much you would like to contribute to them.

- Prepare your Will, ensure it is legally binding and consult your local scholars if necessary.

- Ensure that a member of the family knows about all of your finances, direct debits, standing orders, bills which need to be paid regularly, from which accounts they get paid etc. This will ensure there is no added pressure on the family if you pass away and they are unaware of the household finances.

So you can see from the above that this could be a complicated exercise if you own a lot of assets, but it is a necessary exercise. It may also be very sensitive, as you may have to consult family members about assets, especially if you live in a household with an extended family.

Some time ago I prepared a short booklet called 'Testators Asset & Finance Identifier' regarding this subject. I have included it in Appendix C.

Each person should fill this in and keep it with their Islamic Will, updating it as and when necessary.

An Islamic Will Template has also been given in Appendix B.

Question: What is the ruling on purchasing and preparing your own grave in your lifetime?

Answer: It is permissible. However, it is worth noting that no one knows the place of his/her death.[5]

Question: How can a person who has embraced Islām and lives with non-Muslim family members, or is a Muslim who is in a relationship with a non-Muslim, ensure their burial takes place according to Islamic Rites?

Answer: Many Islamic Wills will have a section stipulating the requirement of an Islamic burial. Another option is for them to sign a Statutory Declaration in the presence of 2 witnesses. This Declaration should be given to their next of kin and also to anyone else who would be able to present it at the time of their death. It can also be given to their Hospital/Hospice/Care Home if applicable.

A Sample Statutory Declaration can be found in Appendix A.

---

[5] https://islamicportal.co.uk/preparing-own-grave-whilst-alive/

WHAT TO DO WHEN A PERSON IS PASSING AWAY

We may at some time come across a situation where we witness another Muslim person passing away. It could be an expected death after an illness, or it could be sudden.

It is necessary that we aid the person in this difficult time by making their last few moments correct. Therefore there are certain guidelines we must follow.

Question: What are the Physical Signs of a person who is nearing death?

Answer: A person may have been ill for some time, so it may be difficult to determine if their actual time of passing away has arrived. Some of the signs of a person who is approaching death are as follows:

- The quickening of the breath
- Nose becomes bent
- Temples subside
- Body becomes cold
- Body becomes weak

It is important that we recognize these signs, so we make the correct preparations including calling close family. The time just before death, is known as *Sakarāt*.

Question: What is the person called who is about to pass away?

Answer: The person who is about to pass away and on whom the signs of death can be clearly seen, is called a *Muḥtaḍar*. This is taken from the Arabic word 'Ḥaḍarah' which means to be present. The reason why they are called a *Muḥtaḍar* is because death is present, or the Angels of Death are present.

Question: Who should be present when the person is passing away?

Answer: The family members of the *Muḥtaḍar* should be present. If they have no family, then the friends should be there and then the neighbours and members of the community. If we have been told that death is imminent, we must ensure that they are not alone during their final moments in this world.

It is common practise in some communities that when we find out someone is about to pass away, many people attend the house or hospital. We must remember that the Hospitals have rules in place which we must adhere to and ensure we control our emotions at this sensitive time.

Many times the room in which the *Muḥtaḍar* is present is very small. We should allow the close family members to be present at that time and people who would know what to do from an Islamic perspective whilst the *Muḥtaḍar* is passing away.

Any person who is in the state of ritual impurity (Janābah) should not be present. If they would like to be present, then they should have a ritual bath (Ghusl)

Question: When a person is passing away, is it permissible for a woman in menses to sit in the same room and make dhikr (remembrance) of Allāh?

Answer: Our Ḥanafī jurists have differed regarding a woman in menses sitting near a person who is passing away. Some jurists say this is permissible. Others suggest that she should not remain there due to her impure state. However, this appears to be advisory and not a compulsory ruling. For this reason, if the woman is a close family member or associate of the person, there is no harm and she will not be sinful if she remains in the room. She should supplicate and undertake dhikr (remembrance) of Allāh سُبْحَانَهُوَتَعَالَ and preferably avoid sitting very close to the deceased.

It should be noted that the impurity of a woman in menses is Ḥukmī (abstract/ritual), not Ḥaqīqī (actual). This is understood from the Ḥadīth of Rasūlullāh صَلَّىٱللَّهُعَلَيْهِوَسَلَّمَ when he said to ʿĀi'shah رَضِيَٱللَّهُعَنْهَا (d. 58/678), "Your menstruation is not in your hand" (Ṣaḥīḥ Muslim, 298). Rasūlullāh صَلَّىٱللَّهُعَلَيْهِوَسَلَّمَ would also recline in her lap when she was menstruating, and recite the Qurʾān (Ṣaḥīḥ al-Bukhārī, 297). Accordingly, there is no need to be strict regarding this during times of grief.[6]

---

[6] https://islamicportal.co.uk/can-woman-in-menses-sit-near-the-deceased-and-wash-the-deceased/

Question: In which position should we lay the person before they pass away?

Answer: Firstly, if moving the *Muḥtaḍar* causes discomfort then it is best to leave them as they are. With regards to the position in which they should be laid, there are two opinions.

Firstly, lie them on their right side facing the Qiblah, as this is the way they will be laid in the grave. Try putting pillows under the left side of the *Muḥtaḍar* so the whole body is resting towards the right and Qiblah. The evidence for turning a person towards the Qiblah can be found in the Ḥadīth below:

عَنْ يَحْيَى بْنِ عَبْدِ اللَّهِ بْنِ أَبِى قَتَادَةَ عَنْ أَبِيهِ أَنَّ النَّبِيَّ صَلَّى اللهُ عَلَيْهِ وَسَلَّمَ حِينَ قَدِمَ الْمَدِينَةَ سَأَلَ عَنِ الْبَرَاءِ بْنِ مَعْرُورٍ فَقَالُوا: تُوُفِّيَ وَأَوْصَى بِثُلُثِهِ لَكَ يَا رَسُولَ اللَّهِ وَأَوْصَى أَنْ يُوَجَّهَ إِلَى الْقِبْلَةِ لَمَّا احْتُضِرَ فَقَالَ رَسُولُ اللَّهِ صَلَّى اللهُ عَلَيْهِ وَسَلَّمَ "أَصَابَ الْفِطْرَةَ"[7]

---

[7] Al-Mustadrak Al-Ḥākim 1305

Abu Qatādah ﷺ narrates from his father that when the Prophet ﷺ came to Madīnah, he asked about Barā' ibn Ma'rūr ﷺ. They said that he had passed away and made a bequest of one third of his wealth for you oh Prophet of Allāh and also made a bequest that he should be faced towards the Qiblah when he is close to death. The Prophet ﷺ then said, "He has attained fiṭrah", which means pure nature i.e. he has passed away on the natural disposition - Islām.

The evidence for turning a person on the right side can be found in the Ḥadīth below:

عَنْ سَعْدِ بْنِ عُبَيْدَةَ قَالَ: حَدَّثَنِي الْبَرَاءُ بْنُ عَازِبٍ رَضِيَ اللَّهُ عَنْهُمَا قَالَ: قَالَ لِي رَسُولُ اللَّهِ صَلَّى اللهُ عَلَيْهِ وَسَلَّمَ: " إِذَا أَتَيْتَ مَضْجَعَكَ فَتَوَضَّأْ وَضُوءَكَ لِلصَّلَاةِ ثُمَّ اضْطَجِعْ عَلَى شِقِّكَ الْأَيْمَنِ وَقُلْ: اللَّهُمَّ أَسْلَمْتُ نَفْسِى إِلَيْكَ وَفَوَّضْتُ أَمْرِى إِلَيْكَ وَأَلْجَأْتُ ظَهْرِى إِلَيْكَ رَهْبَةً وَرَغْبَةً إِلَيْكَ لَا مَلْجَأً وَلاَ مَنْجَا مِنْكَ إِلَّا إِلَيْكَ

آمَنْتُ بِكِتَابِكَ الَّذِى أَنْزَلْتَ وَبِنَبِيِّكَ الَّذِى أَرْسَلْتَ فَإِنْ مُتَّ مُتَّ عَلَى الفِطْرَةِ⁸

In the above Ḥadīth narrated by Barā' ibn ʿĀzib ﷺ, Rasūlullāh ﷺ mentions a number of actions a person should do before they go to sleep, one of which is to lay on the right-hand side. Rasūlullāh ﷺ further mentions that if you pass away that night, you have passed away on fitrah.

The second opinion which can be found in the books of fiqh is to lay the *Muḥtaḍar* on their back with their feet in the direction of the Qiblah. The head should be raised slightly so they are facing towards the Qiblah and not towards the sky.

In this position, there are several benefits mentioned as follows:

- It is easier for the soul to leave the body
- The eyes of the deceased can be easily closed if needed, once they have passed away
- A cloth can be easily tied around the head of the deceased to keep the jaw closed
- The limbs of the *Muḥtaḍar* will be in a straight position

---

⁸ Ṣaḥīḥ al-Bukhārī 6311

So from the above, we can determine that the *Muḥtaḍar* should be laid if possible, on their right-hand side facing the Qiblah or on their back with their feet facing towards the Qiblah with their head slightly raised.

Question: What should we pray near the dying person?

Answer: As per the Ḥadīth below, it is recommended that Surah Yāsīn be read in their presence.

عَنْ مَعْقِلِ بْنِ يَسَارٍ قَالَ

قَالَ النَّبِيُّ صَلَّى اللَّهُ عَلَيْهِ وَسَلَّمَ اقْرَءُوا يس عَلَى مَوْتَاكُمْ[9]

Maʿqal ibn Yasār ﷺ narrates that the Prophet ﷺ said "Recite Yāsīn over your Dying"

The other opinion for this Ḥadīth is that the word 'Mawtākum' is taken as the literal meaning, so it means "Recite Yāsīn over your dead".

The Talqīn

Question: What is Talqīn?

Answer: As per the Ḥadīth below, Talqīn is the action to remind the person who is passing away of the kalimah.

---

[9] Sunan Abū Dāwūd 3121

عَنْ أَبِى سَعِيدٍ

عَنِ النَّبِيّ صَلَّى اللَّهُ عَلَيْهِ وَسَلَّمَ قَالَ لَقِّنُوا مَوْتَاكُمْ لَا إِلَهَ إِلَّا اللَّهُ

10

Abū Saʿīd ؓ narrates that the Prophet ﷺ said
"Perform the Talqīn for your dead with Lā ilāha illallāh"

In this Ḥadīth the meaning of the word "your dead" are the people who are in the state of 'Sakarāt' i.e. about to die in a short while and the signs of death have become apparent

How to perform the Talqīn

A person should sit near the *Muḥtaḍar* and read the kalimah in a voice loud enough so that they can hear. When the *Muḥtaḍar* hears the kalimah, Inshā'Allāh they will also recite it.

We should not instruct the Muḥtaḍar to recite it, but keep on reciting it until the *Muḥtaḍar* recites the kalimah as well. Sometimes the *Muḥtaḍar* could be going through extreme pain so they may refuse to recite the kalimah if we keep on forcing them. Once the *Muḥtaḍar* has recited the kalimah, the people reciting the Talqīn should remain silent. This is to ensure that the last words the *Muḥtaḍar* recites, are the kalimah.

---

[10] Jāmiʿ al-Tirmidhī 898

If we start to discuss worldly matters and the *Muḥtaḍar* gets drawn into the conversation, the Talqīn will have to be repeated. Also if the *Muḥtaḍar* themselves start to talk about any worldly matters, we should repeat the Talqīn again.

Note: If the *Muḥtaḍar* recites any Dhikr or says any religious thing after reciting the kalimah, the Talqīn does not have to be recited.

Furthermore, what if the *Muḥtaḍar* does not recite the Kalimah but uttered some other words or remained silent, what does this mean? This question has been answered by Maulānā Yūsuf Shabbir.

Question: A brother during his last moments due to extreme discomfort was uttering "Allāh, Allāh, Allāh" and passed away. Will it be considered that he died as a believer even though he did not recite the full Kalimah?

Answer: Any Muslim who passes away is regarded a believer even if he does not read anything before his demise. If someone said the Shahādah during his life, and continued to believe in this, he is regarded a believer even if he does not read the Shahādah during his demise.

In addition, if a believer has said "Allāh, Allāh" or similar words just before his demise, this Inshā' Allāh is a positive sign and an extra indicator that he has left the world with Īmān (faith). It also provides a positive summary of his life, because actions are according to their final deeds. A person who remembers Allāh during this difficult moment is commendable. May Allāh Almighty grant us all death upon Īmān.[11]

What to do when the Muḥtaḍar passes away

When the *Muḥtaḍar* has passed away, if the eyes are still open, they should be closed as per the actions of Rasūlullāh ﷺ.

عَنْ أُمِّ سَلَمَةَ قَالَتْ

دَخَلَ رَسُولُ اللَّهِ صَلَّى اللَّهُ عَلَيْهِ وَسَلَّمَ عَلَى أَبِي سَلَمَةَ وَقَدْ شَقَّ بَصَرَهُ فَأَغْمَضَهُ [12]

"Umme Salamah ﵂ narrates that the Prophet ﷺ entered when Abū Salamah ﵄ had passed away and his eyes were open, so he closed them."

After closing the eyes, close the jaw gently and keep it in place by tying a strip of cloth around the head and tie it firmly at the top.

Straighten all of the limbs gently but do not force them. Sometimes if the body has been through certain conditions, the limbs will not straighten and

---

[11] https://islamicportal.co.uk/saying-allah-at-the-time-of-demise/

[12] Ṣaḥīḥ Muslim 2711

forcing them could cause them to fracture or break. Place the legs together and tie the ankles together with a strip of cloth so they stay in place.

Remove all jewellery from the body, especially for women such as rings, necklaces, earing's, nose piercings etc.

If the person has passed away in a Hospital, the staff will assist you. You can request that they remove all of the tubes/catheters etc. and bandage any open wounds. They will also place the deceased inside a body bag, ready for transportation.

THE IMPORTANCE OF AN EARLY BURIAL

Our Religion of Islām provides advice for us on all aspects concerning our life. From birth, right through to death. Sometimes our religious Rites may be not in conformance with the practices of the country we live in. For example in the UK, the normal time for a burial or cremation after the time of death could be several weeks. For Muslims, we should try and ensure we bury our deceased as soon as possible.

The reason why we must bury our deceased has been explained on Islamic Portal. The section below has been taken from the answer.[13]

As Muslims, our religion of Islām places great emphasis on burying the deceased as soon as possible. Part of honouring a deceased is to arrange the burial as soon as possible (al-Madhkal, 3:236). There are many narrations which emphasise this, one of which is below.

عَنْ أَبِي هُرَيْرَةَ رضى الله عنه عَنِ النَّبِيِّ صلى الله عليه وسلم قَالَ " أَسْرِعُوا بِالْجَنَازَةِ فَإِنْ تَكُ صَالِحَةً فَخَيْرٌ تُقَدِّمُونَهَا {إِلَيْهِ} وَإِنْ يَكُ سِوَى ذَلِكَ فَشَرٌّ تَضَعُونَهُ عَنْ رِقَابِكُمْ "[14]

---

¹³ https://islamicportal.co.uk/importance-of-early-burial/

¹⁴ Ṣaḥīḥ al-Bukhārī, 1315

Rasūlullāh ﷺ said

"Hurry up with the dead body for if it was righteous, you are forwarding it to good; and if it was otherwise, then you are putting off an evil thing from your necks"

The famous Ḥanafī jurist ʿAllāmah Sarakhsī (d. ca. 490/1097) explains that if the transfer of the body results in the delay of the burial by a few days, this is sufficient for it to be detestable (Sharḥ al-Siyar al-Kabīr, 1:236).

Therefore, under normal circumstances, it is of great importance that the deceased is buried as soon as possible. If there is a legitimate reason for the delay, for example, a post-mortem or MRI scan is necessary to ascertain the cause of death, this is excused.

BURYING THE DECEASED ABROAD

It is the practise in certain communities to send the body of the deceased to other countries for burial. This practise is not recommended unless there is a justifiable reason. This issue has also been discussed by Maulānā Yūsuf Shabbir. Some of the reasons why the body should not be transferred are mentioned below:[15]

1. It contravenes the emphasis Islām places on burying the deceased as soon as possible as mentioned in the previous chapter.

2. Our religion is simple and avoids extravagance and unnecessary costs. This is reflected in the simplicity of the Kafan, the cloth used to shroud the deceased. The ccst of transporting the deceased abroad is at least a few thousand pounds. Spending this money without a valid Islamic basis is not permissible.

   Allāh سُبْحَانَهُوَتَعَالَى says in verse 7 of Sūrah Al-Aʿrāf "Do be not extravagant, surely He does not like the extravagant". Instead, the deceased would benefit if these funds are utilised for charitable projects on behalf of the deceased. The reward of this would reach and benefit the deceased as mentioned in various narrations (*Ṣaḥīḥ Muslim, 1631*). If we are truly concerned about our beloved family members, Ṣadaqah is one of the most effective ways of benefiting them.

3. Many people believe that there is some virtue or significance attached to burying the deceased in their birth place or place of origin or with

---

[15] https://islamicportal.co.uk/burying-a-deceased-abroad/

their forefathers.   There is no basis for this belief. It is therefore necessary to challenge this belief by avoiding this practise and encouraging others to avoid it.

It is worth noting that there is virtue attached to passing away and being buried in the blessed city of Madīnah, as affirmed in various narrations (Ṣaḥīḥ al-Bukhārī, 1890; Muwaṭṭaʾ, 1678; Sunan al-Tirmidhī, 3917). However, in the time of the Prophet ﷺ and the time of the Companions, the general practice was to bury the deceased in the location where they passed away. This includes the martyrs who were buried in Uḥud and not in the Cemetery of Baqīᶜ.

Many Companions passed away in the surrounding regions of Makkah and Madīnah, but their bodies were not brought to Makkah or Madīnah for burial. For example, the mother of believers, Maymūnah ﵂ (d. 51/671-2) passed away in a place known as Sarif, approximately ten miles from Makkah. She was buried in Sarif and not in the blessed city of Makkah. Similarly, we find that there are many graves of the Companions all over the world. Their bodies were not transported back to Makkah or Madīnah or the capitals of the Muslim world. It is worth noting that according to one narration from Imām Shāfiᶜī ﵀ (d. 204/820), if a person passes away in close proximity to Makkah or Madīnah or al-Quds, it is desirable for the body to be transferred there (Rawḍah al-Ṭālibīn, 2: 143). However, the statement of the mother of believers ᶜĀʾishah ﵂ (d. 58/678) regarding the burial of her brother whose body was transported to Makkah and the general practice of the Muslims suggests that it is preferable for the deceased to be buried in the location of their death.

4. It is a legal requirement in many countries to embalm the body before transportation. The embalmment process consists of four stages. This includes the corpse undergoing treatment and being filled with chemical preservatives including alcoholic solvents. This process, again without a valid reason, is prohibited and violates the sanctity of a deceased person. In addition to this, much of the deceased's body is kept uncovered during this process. This again, without a valid reason, violates the sanctity of the deceased which contravenes Islamic teachings. The Prophet ﷺ has affirmed the importance of honouring and respecting the sanctity of a deceased person as reflected in the following Ḥadīth,

$$\text{" } كَسْرُ عَظْمِ الْمَيِّتِ كَكَسْرِهِ حَيًّا \text{ "}^{[16]}$$

"Breaking the bones of the deceased is like breaking his bones when he is alive"

Finally, it is worth noting that transferring the body within a region is permissible if there is a need to do so although ʿAllāmah Sarakhsī رحمه الله (d. ca. 490/1097) has specified that the distance should not exceed one or two miles (*Radd al-Muḥtār*, 6: 428; *Sharḥ al-Siyar al-Kabīr*, 1: 236; *Fatāwā Farīdiyyah*, 3: 284; *Fatāwā Maḥmūdiyyah*, 13: 259).

---

[16] Sunan Ibn Mājah 1616

Other scholars have permitted this on the condition that the sanctity of the corpse is not violated and that it does not start to emit odour (*al-Furūʿ*, 3: 327; *Ḥāshiyah al-Dasūqī*, 4: 165).

In conclusion, it is prohibited in the absence of a valid reason to transfer the body of a deceased person from the UK to another country, such as India or Pakistan.

LEGAL PREPARATION

At the time of writing, the advice given in this section is correct. However there is currently a program called the 'NHS medical examiner system' being rolled out by the NHS. This system will introduce a new level of scrutiny whereby all deaths will be subject to either a medical examiner's scrutiny or a coroner's investigation. Once this system has been implemented, Inshā'Allāh, this section will be updated accordingly.

Before a burial can take place, there are certain legal requirements regarding documentation. There are a number of forms which must be obtained before permission for the burial is granted.

The deceased will have either passed away at home or at a hospital. There will be different scenarios as to whether the person will need to have a post mortem or not.

Another important factor is to keep your local GP informed if the person is passing away at home. This will help in obtaining the 'Cause of Death' Certificate and potentially remove any possible delays.

Sometimes, in trying to get the deceased buried as soon as possible we can cause inconvenience to the various associations which are aiding us in the burial, like the Doctors, Undertakers, Registrar's Office etc. We have to understand that they have a protocol they need to work under and standard procedures they need to follow. We have to try our best to get the burial done as soon as possible but under no circumstances should we expect any of them to break protocol and assist us at the first instance.

This section gives information on the general procedure in the United Kingdom. This may vary for certain communities, so it is recommended that the family of the deceased confirm what their local procedure will be. Many times, there are local funeral committees or members of the community who are familiar with the burial process so it would be a good idea to engage with them as soon as needed.

Documents

MCCD – Medical Certificate of Cause of Death

This document is normally issued by the Doctor (GP or Hospital Doctor) and must be presented at the Registrar's office. If the form is being filled in immediately after the death and no post mortem is necessary, make sure to tell the doctor to fill in the form accordingly so the death is not referred to the coroner.

Certificate of Burial (Green Form)

This document is issued by the Registrar so the deceased can be buried. The burial cannot take place until this form has been given to the burial authority. The Registrar will not charge for this form.

Death Certificate

This is a certificated copy of the entry in the Death Register and issued by the Registrar. The family of the deceased can use this as evidence for making claims for the assets of the deceased. There will be a charge for this form.

Interment Form

This form is given to the Bereavement Services so they can prepare the grave accordingly. This form will contain information including the size of the coffin being used for the burial. Even if a coffin is not being used, you will need to supply them with details of the size of the casket which will be used to transport the deceased.

Please consult your local Muslim Funeral Committee who may have copies of the Interment form and may also help to fill them out.

Burial Times

This will vary for different cities depending on what arrangements the community has with the local councils. We must remember when organizing the bathing (Ghusl) and the Janāzah Ṣalāh, the time it will take to move the body to the cemetery and complete the burial process. Each burial will be given a fixed time slot, so it is necessary that the mourners arrive on time and complete the burial within the allotted time frame.

Scenario 1 – Person passes away at home, expected death, cause of death is known, no post mortem needed.

1. Contact the family doctor. If this is out of hours, then it might be difficult. Ensure you have the number of the surgery at hand and get in touch with them as soon as they open. If the doctor had visited the person in his/her final illness and had seen the deceased AFTER death or within 14 days of the death, they may issue a 'Cause of Death' Certificate. If for any reason the Doctor cannot issue the certificate, then the death will be reported to the Duty Coroner.

Question: What if we can't get hold of the family doctor?

Answer: If you can't get hold of the family doctor then you should inform the doctor's practise that you require a 'Cause of Death' Certificate. They will then inform you of what needs to be done

2. Contact a member of the Local Muslim Burial Committee. They will help you with your legal preparations and answer any queries you may have. Their names can be obtained from your local Masjid. The Local Muslim Burial Committee may be classed as the Undertaker for the Funeral.

   Confirm the local legal process with them and which departments you will need to personally visit and which departments they can liaise with, on your behalf i.e. Bereavement Services. They may also have copies of the Interment Form which they will help fill in and pass onto the Bereavement Services.

Also confirm the Islamic arrangements, as follows:

- If they have provision to store the body of the deceased (cold room)
- Do they have facilities to perform the Ghusl?
- Do they have anyone to assist in the Ghusl if necessary?
- Can they provide the shroud (Kafan)?
- Do they provide a place for people to come and pay their respects etc.

3. The next stage is to contact the local Register Office to register the death. An appointment can be arranged by telephone. If there is not much time, then it would be better if someone attended the Register Office in person and see if the relevant documentation can be obtained. Only the following people are allowed to register the death:

- A relative of the deceased
- Someone present at the death
- The occupier of the house, or hospital, if he or she knew of the death
- Another person living at the house if he or she knew of the death
- The person making the arrangements with the funeral directors

The death must be registered within 5 days. The 'Cause of Death' Certificate should then be taken to the Register Office along with the following documents/information.

- Date and place of death
- The Medical Card of the deceased if available
- Name and surname of the deceased

- Maiden surname, if the deceased was a woman who had married
- Date and place of birth
- Occupation
- Name and occupation of spouse/civil partner, where the deceased was married or had a civil partnership.
- Usual address
- Whether the deceased was in receipt of a pension or allowance from public funds
- If the deceased was married or had a civil partner, the date of birth of the surviving widow, widower or civil partner.

The Registrar will then issue 2 Certificates as follows:

'Certificate of Burial' (Green Form)

This is a Green Certificate and has to be handed to the Bereavement Services/Undertaker so they can give authorisation to proceed with the burial.

'Certificate of Registration of Death' (Death Certificate)

This certificate may take longer to process so may be posted or another appointment can be arranged. This certificate will be issued to the deceased person's next of kin to process any necessary claims and close down any bank accounts etc.

4. Once the 'Certificate of Burial' Certificate has been obtained from the Registrar, you will need to contact your local Bereavement Services to arrange the Burial. If your Local Muslim burial committee provided you

the Interment form, then you can submit it to them at this time. In some cases the Interment form may have already been faxed to the Bereavement Services or sent digitally to them by your local burial committee.

If you haven't been given an Interment form, then you will have to inform the Bereavement Services of the size of the grave you require, whether the grave will be filled in by the mourners, whether they need to provide the tools to fill the grave etc.

Once this process has been completed, they will give you a time and date for the burial.

There will also be a cost involved for the burial. Again, costs can be obtained from the local Muslim Funeral Committee.

If for any reason the burial is delayed, then there may also be a surcharge. We must allow enough time to obtain the relevant documentation before we bury the deceased, so keep this in mind.

Out of Hours

If the person has passed away during the weekend or holiday period when the Register Office is closed, then certain provisions may be in place depending on your Local Muslim Funeral Committees arrangement with the local authority.

Scenario 2 – Person passes away at home and cause of Death is unknown

If a person passes away suddenly at home, in this instance an ambulance should be called to confirm that the person has indeed passed away. A local doctor can also be called if they are available. If the doctor can determine the cause of death then he/she may issue a Cause of Death Certificate, however further investigation may be needed to determine the cause of death. On this instance, the doctor will inform the police services who in turn will inform the Coroner. The Coroner is normally only needed for the following:

- The deceased was not visited by a doctor or had not seen a doctor in the last 14 days
- The cause of death cannot be determined
- Death was sudden, violent or caused by an accident

Post Mortem

A post-mortem examination, also known as an autopsy, is the examination of a body after death. The aim of a post-mortem is to determine the cause of death.

Post-mortems are carried out by pathologists (doctors who specialize in understanding the nature and causes of disease).

Once the Coroner gets the case, he/she can decide if a post-mortem is needed or not, to help determine the cause of death. The normal procedure for a post mortem is to perform a physical dissection of the body. This can then cause problems when the Ghusl is performed of the deceased.

In some areas there may be an option to have a non-invasive alternative such as a CT/MRI Scan. If it is determined that a post-mortem is necessary, then please check with the Coroner if you can exercise your right to have the alternative. The CT/MRI Scan is preferred to the post mortem as it is a less invasive procedure.

Please remember that the Coroner does not need the permission of the family in order to carry out the procedure. There also maybe delays in performing the procedure. At this time we can inform the Coroner that our religious obligations require us to bury the person as soon as possible, so they can try and get it done as soon as they can. The Coroners in our country are familiar with our requirements and are very accommodating, so they will try their best. Sometimes there will be delays, so we just have to exercise patience and let the process complete.

Once the Coroner has determined the cause of death, they will issue a certificate which they will send to the Registrar. It may also be given to the family or the burial committee to take themselves to the Registrar's Office. This certificate will allow the Registrar to process the necessary documentation needed for the burial.

The Green certificate – Certificate of Disposal will be issued by the Registrar and this must then be given to the Bereavement Services/Undertaker as mentioned before.

The Certificate of Registration of Death may be issued at a later date. It is not needed to process the burial.

Inquest

If the Coroner decides that there is still further investigation needed to determine the cause of death or if there were other factors involved like violence or an accident, then an inquest will be held. This should not delay the burial process unless further examination of the body is required. There may be instances where a second post mortem is required.

Scenario 3 – Person Passes away in Hospital and cause of death is known

1. The Doctor will issue the Cause of Death Certificate if the cause of death is known. There should be no need to perform the post mortem however if the Doctor wishes to perform a hospital post- mortem, they must obtain permission from the nearest relative, if the dying person did not give consent prior to their death.
2. Follow the same steps as in Scenario 1

Scenario 4 – Person Passes away in Hospital and cause of death is unknown

The doctor will refer the case to the Coroner. The steps will be the same as in Scenario 2

At the Cemetery - The Burial Process

The Bereavement Officer at the Cemetery will meet the procession at the gate and inform them of the location of the grave and where to park. There may be instances where due to tight schedules, it has been agreed that the Green Form and the Interment Form be handed to the Officer.

The burial will then commence. The grave will be filled by the mourners as per our Islamic Practice. There may be a need for the Undertaker to remove the Shoring's of the Grave. Once they have been removed, the grave can then be filled.

Once the grave has been filled, the mourners will leave.

Note: If the mourners wish to fill the grave, then ensure they have the relevant tools necessary, picks, spades etc. if they are not provided by the Cemetery Staff.

Note: Please park in the designated areas and do not block any roads or drives

LEGAL PROCESS – QUICK LOOKUP CHART

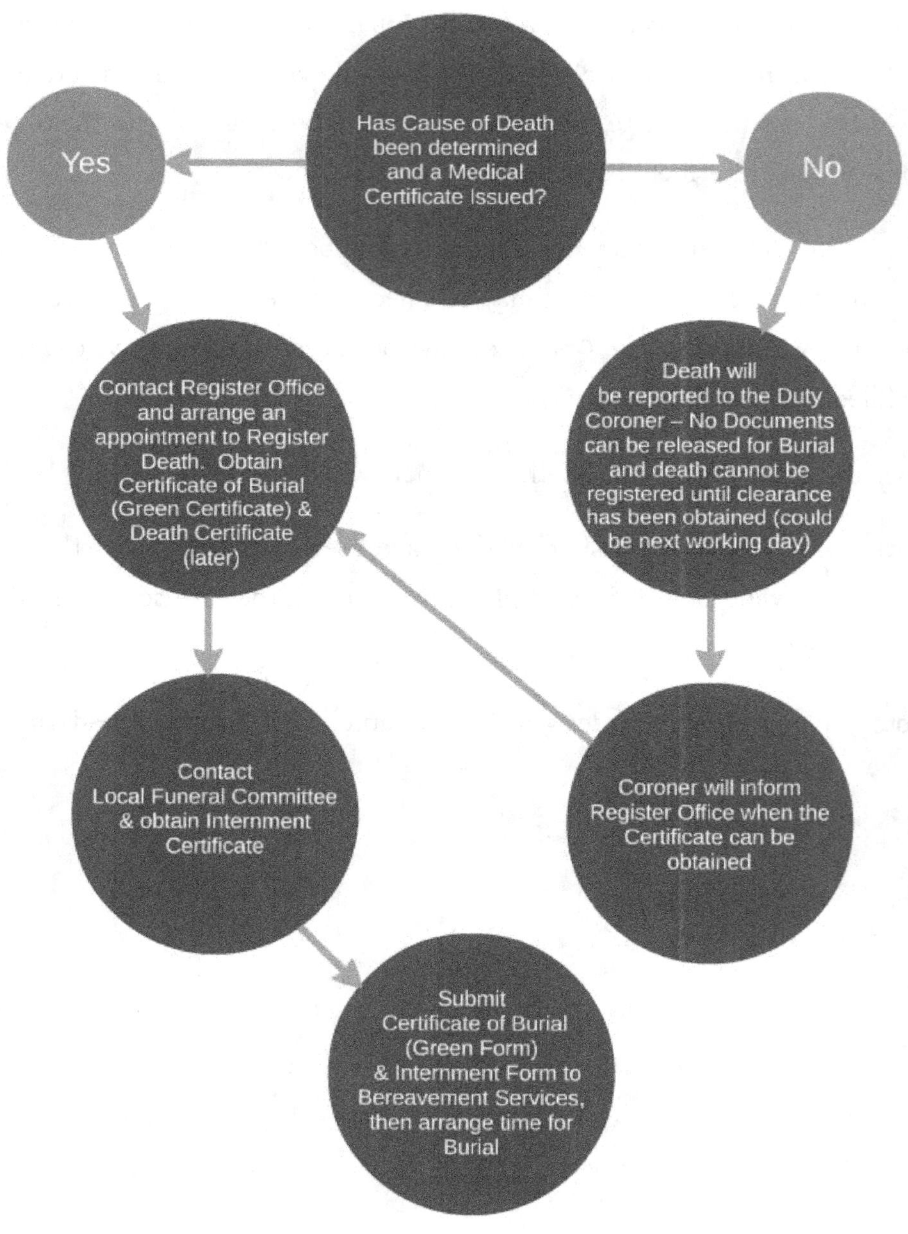

GHUSL OF THE DECEASED

Question: Why is Ghusl needed for the Deceased?

Answer: The wisdom behind bathing the deceased is that, Allāh سُبْحَانَهُوَتَعَالَ servant who is leaving this world and going to the afterlife, Sharīʿah has given the command that the body should be sent with honour and respect. There is no better way for the deceased to be sent with respect then to bathe them, make them clean and clothe them in clean sheets.

What to do with the body before the Ghusl

Once the person has passed away, the body parts have been tied up and all jewellery removed, the next stage would be to prepare for the Ghusl.

Whilst the preparation is going on, who is allowed to stay with the body? Are we allowed to touch it? What do we pray? These are just some of the questions which crop up time and time again.

Question: Can the Qur'ān be recited in the presence of a deceased, before he/she has been washed?

Answer: Our jurists have a difference of opinion regarding the recitation of the Qur'ān in the presence of the deceased before he/she has been washed. Some scholars suggest that this is disliked until the deceased has been washed whilst some others suggest that it is permissible except when the deceased is being washed.

According to the preferred view, the Qur'ān can be recited before the deceased is washed as long as there are no visible impurities. As the deceased in our country is generally covered, there is no harm in reciting the Qur'ān before the deceased is washed. The deceased should be washed as soon as possible, but it is recognised that sometimes there can be delays beyond the control of the family.[17]

Note: There is no difference of opinion regarding the permissibility of reciting the Qur'ān from another room or elsewhere. It is a common misconception that the Qur'ān cannot be recited at all until the deceased has been washed.

Question: Are close family allowed to touch the body? Is there any sin in kissing the body of the deceased?

Answer: There is no harm in touching the body of the deceased, also there is no harm in kissing the deceased (both only for those who are allowed). When a person passes away, the body becomes unclean and Ghusl is necessary, without the Ghusl, the Janāzah Ṣalāh is not permissible. The uncleanliness is Ḥukmī (Unseen Uncleanliness) not Ḥaqīqī (Visible Uncleanliness) therefore the visible part of the body is clean.

The Ḥadīth below shows one occasion when Rasūlullāh ﷺ kissed the head of one of his companions.

---

[17] https://islamicportal.co.uk/recitation-of-the-quran-after-demise/

عَنْ عَائِشَةَ أَنَّ النَّبِيَّ صَلَّى اللَّهُ عَلَيْهِ وَسَلَّمَ قَبَّلَ عُثْمَانَ بْنَ مَظْعُونٍ وَهُوَ مَيِّتٌ وَهُوَ يَبْكِي أَوْ قَالَ عَيْنَاهُ تَذْرِفَانِ [18]

"'Āi'shah ﵂ narrates that the Prophet ﷺ kissed 'Uthmān ibn Maz'ūn ﵁ and he had passed away and the Prophet ﷺ was crying or said that his eyes were flowing"

Question: Is a non-maḥram male or female allowed to see the deceased?

Answer: Just like whilst the person was living, purdah was observed, it should be observed in the same manner after the person passes away. Therefore any males should not see the face or body of a non maḥram female and vice versa.

Where to keep the body between the time of passing away and performing Ghusl

If there is going to be no delay in performing the burial and the Ghusl, then it is recommended that the body be moved to the place of the Ghusl at the correct time. If there is a risk that the funeral could get delayed for any reason, then it is recommended that the body be moved to a Mortuary.

---

[18] Jāmiʿ al-Tirmidhī 910

Nowadays many Masājid have mortuary facilities including cold rooms where the bodies can be stored.

The reason for moving the body is that after a short while, Rigor Mortis starts to set it on the body of the deceased person. Rigor Mortis literally means 'stiffness of death'. The limbs of the deceased become stiff and hard to move. There will also be other signs of decay and decomposition if the body is left in state for a while and this can cause distress to the family. Therefore if there is going to be significant delay, it would be best if the body is left in the mortuary until the time of the Ghusl.

Preparation for Ghusl & Shrouding

Before a person is buried in Islām, they should be bathed and shrouded according to the Sunnah of Rasūlullāh ﷺ. The shroud should be prepared before the Ghusl, so as soon as the body is ready there is no delay in putting on its shroud.

Preparing the Shroud

You can use any clean material, preferably white for the Kafan or shroud. You will need approximately 15 yards of material. The local Masjid will normally have a stock of this and there should be an ʿĀlim (scholar) or Burial Committee representative to aid in the shrouding and the Ghusl process of the deceased.

The Basic Rule of the Kafan is that a person can wear as a Kafan any cloth which was permissible for them in their lifetime.

Note: It is not permissible to use a shroud made out of silk for men or women as it is considered extravagance. The Kafan should not be too extravagant i.e. made from expensive material and of a larger size or too miserly where the cloth is ripped and torn or is of a smaller size than recommended.

Note: The cost of the shroud should come from the wealth of the deceased however it is permissible for the relatives to also pay for it. If the deceased did not have enough money to pay for the shroud, then responsibility will fall on the guardian. There may be some situations where the guardian cannot also afford it in which case the responsibility used to go to the 'baitul māl' and thereafter the family of the deceased.

Nowadays many local burial committees raise funds from the community to cover the cost of burial, which cannot be afforded by the family of the deceased, or the deceased had no next of kin.

Note: It is permissible to have one's own shroud prepared before they pass away.

The Shroud for the Male and Female are different. The size of the shroud will depend on the size of the person, but some average sizes have been given below.

	Description	Male l x w	Female l x w
Lifāfah	Frome above head to below feet	8ft x 5ft	8ft x 5ft
Sina'Band	From below armpits to the thighs	Not Needed	4ft by 5ft
Izār (Loin Cloth)	From the head to the feet	6ft by 5ft	6ft by 5ft
Qamīs (Shirt)	Folded in half, from shoulders to below the knees	8ft by 5ft (folded 4ft x 5ft)	8ft by 5ft (folded 4ft x 5ft)
Orhni (Scarf)	Covering the head and hair	Not Needed	4ft by 2ft

Three Strips of cloth will also be needed to tie the shroud afterwards.

Preparing the Qamīs (Shirt)

All of the Shrouds will be cut as rectangles, however the sheet for the Qamīs will have to have an extra cut to allow it to be put on the body of the deceased. The sheet for the Qamīs should be folded in two from the top down and then a cut made at the top in the shape of a 'T'. This will allow the sheet to be folded over the body of the deceased.'

A diagram of how the Qamīs should be cut can be seen as follows:

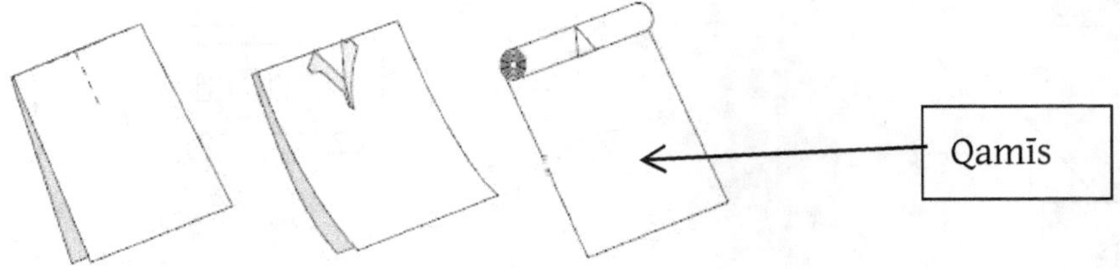

Laying the Shroud

Once all the sheets have been cut to size, they should be laid in the correct order so the body can be placed on the Kafan right after the Ghusl.

For a Male, the 3 strips of cloth will be laid first then the Lifāfah, then the Izār, then the Qamīs as shown below

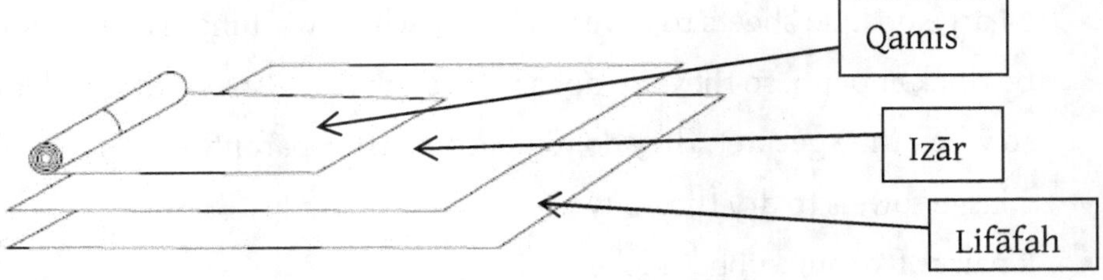

The Qamīs will be folded up at the top so it can but put over the body of the deceased.

For a Female, the 3 strips of cloth will be laid first, then the Lifāfah, Sina'band, Izār, and Qamīs. The Orhni (Scarf) will be put on later

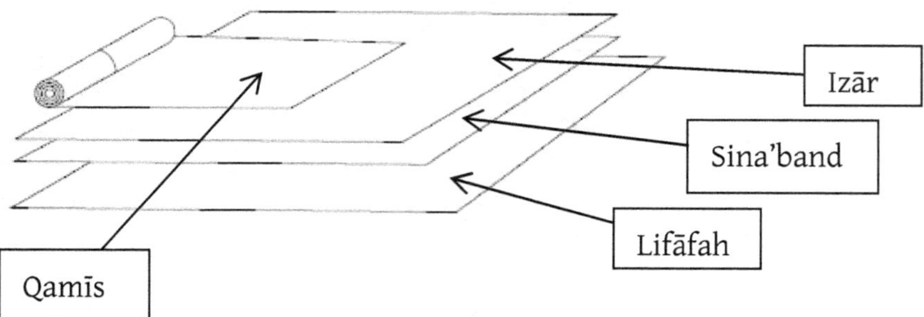

Again, the Qamīs will be folded up at the top so it can but put over the body of the deceased.

Ghusl of the Deceased

Once the shroud has been prepared, the Ghusl of the deceased needs to be performed. For this you will need the following:

- 2 Large opaque sheets to cover the body whilst washing. They should be thick enough, so they are not see through and also of a dark colour so when they get wet, they do not become transparent.
- 2 large towels to dry the body
- 2 pairs of strong rubber gloves
- Normal disposable surgical gloves
- Cotton wool and shampoo
- Soap
- Jugs and bucket
- Bin bags for disposing of rubbish
- Nail polish remover (if required)

Alḥamdulillāh, nowadays many Masājid have special facilities to perform the Ghusl and shrouding of the deceased. They will also have mortuaries where the body can be kept. As the Ghusl of the deceased is not something which is done very often, it is recommended that a local ʿĀlim/ʿĀlimah be consulted or member of the Burial committee tc assist in the Ghusl if needed.

The method of performing the Ghusl of the deceased is very similar to the Ghusl of a living person, however there are a few differences and precautions one must take.

Before we go into the method of the actual Ghusl itself, there are a few Masāil (rulings) which need to be clarified.

- Only females should wash the body of a female
- Only males should wash the body of a male
- Women on menses & washing the deceased: Scholars from all schools of thought suggest that it is preferable for the person washing the deceased to be in the state of purity and ablution. It is therefore preferable for the woman in her menses to avoid bathing the deceased, unless there is a need to do so. If, however, there is a close family member of the deceased who wishes to partake in the washing of the deceased, she should not be stopped. [19]
- A female may wash the body of a minor child.
- If there are no males around to perform the Ghusl for a man or females to give the Ghusl to a woman, then please consult your local ʿĀlim

---

[19] https://islamicportal.co.uk/can-woman-in-menses-sit-near-the-deceased-and-wash-the-deceased/

(Scholar) on the permissibility of which people are allowed to carry out the Ghusl.

Important Facts about the Ghusl

Whilst we are performing the Ghusl, we must take great care in handling the body of the deceased. If the body has undergone a Post Mortem, then there will be a chance that blood will flow from the wounds so extra towels may be needed.

For bathing a male, it is recommended that at least 4 people be present to help bathe and carry the body of the deceased. Depending on the size of the person, more may be needed. In the case of a female, it is recommended that at least 6 women aid in the process.

If a person is not familiar with the procedure, then this booklet will Inshā'Allāh have sufficient information for them to be able to carry out the Ghusl. They can get the help of the local ʿĀlim or brothers/sisters who are familiar with performing Ghusl of the deceased if needed.

To put it simply, the Ghusl will be given in the same method as one takes a bath when becoming pure from Janābat (ritual impurity). Some people are under the false impression that only certain people can give the deceased a bath, this is incorrect as people in the villages and women are also able to give the Ghusl.

The only difference between the Ghusl of the living and the deceased will be whether the mouth is open or closed. If it is closed, then the lips will be cleaned with wet cotton wool with the intention of gargling. If the mouth is open, then the inside will be also cleaned with cotton wool. We must take great care not to pour water into the mouth. In the same way the nose will be cleaned carefully with wet cotton wool with the intentioned of Istinshāq (the action of cleaning the nose in Wuḍū).

Performing the Ghusl

The method described below is a practical and easy way in which people will be able to perform the Ghusl of the deceased. One must remember that the Farā'iḍ, Sunnah and Mustaḥab acts of the Ghusl will be the same for the deceased as it is for the living person.

Instruct all people who are handling the body and bathing it to be extra careful and to not rub the body very hard.

Positioning of the Body during Ghusl

It is permissible that the body be positioned with its legs facing towards the Qiblah or the right-hand side of the body positioned towards Qiblah

Qiblah

Whichever position is convenient is permissible

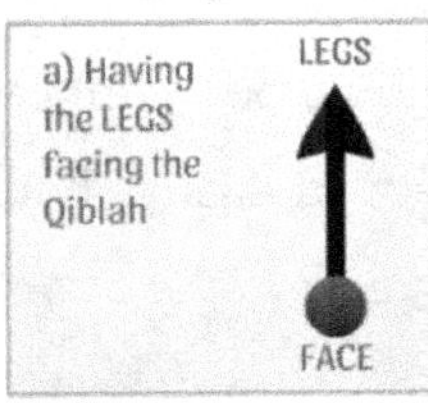

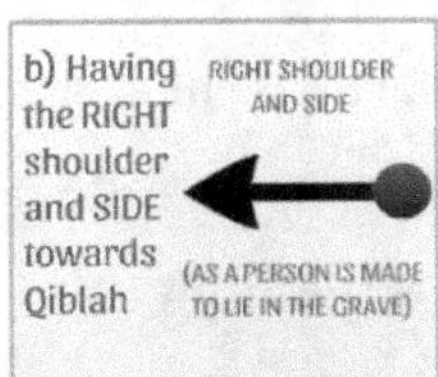

It is recommended that all people who are preforming the Ghusl put on the disposable gloves.

One person should be the main person giving the Ghusl (bath). This should preferably be a close relative. The ʿĀlim or person instructing the Ghusl should also remain close enough to the body to enable them to communicate properly. All other people who are present should aid only when they are asked. The instructions should be left to one person to avoid confusion.

We should also not rush this procedure but take our time and do it properly. Do not leave the Ghusl too late just before the burial so one has to rush it.

The body should be moved carefully and gently onto the washing table.

One person should be nominated to hold the head of the body in place whilst the Ghusl is taking place.

One of the thick covering sheets should then be taken out and 4 people at each corner should hold the sheet just above the body below the head and upto the ankles. The sheet should not be raised too high so the body becomes visible whilst the Ghusl is being carried out and not too low so the washer cannot perform their actions properly.

Note: Remember to use a thick sheet which is not transparent and will not become transparent when water falls on it.

Once the sheet is in place, the next step would be to remove any clothes which are on the body. If they cannot be removed easily then carefully use some scissors to cut away the clothing.

If there are any drips or catheters, then remove these as well. If they cannot be removed, then cut them off as close to the skin as possible. When they are removed, it is possible that this might cause bleeding so use some cotton wool to stop the bleeding. If bleeding doesn't stop, then secure the wool in place with some tape or plaster.

- Remove any dentures and any jewellery which is still on the body
- If there is nail polish on the body, remove this as well using nail polish remover

Once the clothes and any other items have been removed off the body, the body will be ready for the Ghusl.

Prepare the water, if this is done using a shower, check the temperature is not too warm or too cold. If a bucket is being used, ensure that the correct amount of hot and cold water has been mixed. You will also now need a jug if using a bucket.

- Before the body is washed, you must remove any waste from the body of the deceased. One person should put on the strong rubber gloves as they will be cleaning the back passage of the deceased.

  In order to remove the waste, one person should gently but firmly press the stomach. The body should then be tilted to the right side, so the left hand side of the body is raised and the waste should then be washed away with the shower. Use cotton wool to clean the back passage and dispose of the cotton wool in the dustbin bags. Use as much cotton wool as necessary until you are sure it has all been cleaned.

If the person has died recently then the head and shoulders of the body could be raised slightly to try and help clear the waste. If the person has been in cold storage for some time, then this procedure may not be helpful.

Note: If the person died during child birth, or during an operation, or after a post mortem, then this procedure could cause excessive bleeding.

- Wuḍū should then be performed on the body
- Wash the right hand 3 times then then left hand 3 times.
- Wipe the mouth with cotton wool 3 times. If the mouth is open, then clean the inside with wet cotton wool as well not going too far inside.
- Wipe the inside of the nose with cotton wool 3 times
- Wash the face 3 times
- Wash the right arm, up to and including the elbow 3 times, then the left arm
- Perform Masaḥ of the head from the forehead backwards. So the person at the head will place his hands on the forehead of the deceased and wipe them back towards himself.
- Wash the right foot 3 times up to and including the ankles then the left foot.

Note: If the person was in the state of ritual impurity (in need of Ghusl) then the washing of the mouth and nose would be obligatory.

The Wuḍū is now complete.

- The next stage is to wash the hair with shampoo. This is done by one person holding the head in place whilst another washes it. If a woman has her hair in plaits or braids, then it should be undone and parted in two from the middle. The hair should then be placed forward, one part on the right and one part on the left. Once the hair has been shampooed, wash away the shampoo and clean the hair.

- Wet the rest of the body and gently rub soap over the body. Be careful when passing any parts of the body which are wounded or have been bleeding. Start off with the front upper side of the body then tilt the body on the left-hand side so the right-hand side of the body can be washed underneath. Once this has been cleaned then tilt the body to the right so the left-hand side of the body can be washed underneath. Again make sure if there are any signs of waste, then wash these away.

- If there are any wound dressings which are soiled, then remove these, wash the area carefully if possible and then redress if needed.

- The body should then be rinsed 3 times ensuring that all soap, shampoo and waste have been washed away.

- On the last washing, fill a bucket of water and add some camphor. Pour this water over the entire body

Note: The body should be washed an odd number of times. There is a Ḥadīth in Ṣaḥīḥ Muslim where Rasūlullāh ﷺ instructed the women bathing his daughter Zaynab ؓ to wash her an odd number of times, 3 times, 5 times or however many times they deem it necessary. The Ḥadīth also mentions to perform the last washing with camphor mixed in the water.

عَنْ أُمِّ عَطِيَّةَ قَالَتْ لَمَّا مَاتَتْ زَيْنَبُ بِنْتُ رَسُولِ اللَّهِ صَلَّى اللَّهُ عَلَيْهِ وَسَلَّمَ قَالَ لَنَا رَسُولُ اللَّهِ صَلَّى اللَّهُ عَلَيْهِ وَسَلَّمَ اغْسِلْنَهَا وِثْرًا

$$\text{ثَلَاثًا أَوْ خَمْسًا وَاجْعَلْنَ فِي الْخَامِسَةِ كَافُورًا أَوْ شَيْئًا مِنْ كَافُورٍ فَإِذَا غَسَلْتُنَّهَا فَأَعْلِمْنَنِي قَالَتْ فَأَعْلَمْنَاهُ فَأَعْطَانَا حَقْوَهُ وَقَالَ أَشْعِرْنَهَا إِيَّاهُ}^{20}$$

Question:	Why is camphor used?
Answer:	It helps to preserve the body. Insects and other animals which can harm the body do not come close due to the strong smell. Camphor is an inexpensive item which can be used to scent the body. Camphor has a very potent smell so if for any reason the body could not be cleaned properly, the camphor would hide the smell.

Once the Ghusl has finished, gently dry the body with the towels, ensuring that the body is not uncovered. Keep the covering sheet over the body at all times.

After drying the body, apply camphor and perfume on the body. It is better to put on Musk as this is the best perfume.

Question:	Do people who have given the deceased Ghusl need to also perform Ghusl themselves?
Answer:	According to the majority opinion of Jurists, it is Mustaḥab (desirable) for the people who have bathed the deceased to

---

[20] Ṣaḥīḥ Muslim 1559

perform Ghusl themselves. There are 2 advantages in this, firstly there is a possibility that specs of water have touched the body and clothes of the bather which cannot be seen, and these may be unclean. By performing Ghusl, the bather will become clean. Secondly, for people who are not used to bathing the deceased, they could become frightened or get into a state of tension, by taking a bath, it will help them to relax and return to a normal state.

SHROUDING THE BODY

The next stage is to put the Kafan (shroud) on the body. The Shroud should already have been prepared as shown earlier with the 3 binding strips of cloth underneath all of the sheets in reverse order so the Lifafah (outer covering) is at the bottom.

Note: Do not put anything inside the Kafan, whether it is any Duʿāʾs or any verses from the Holy Qurʾān. Also do not write anything on the Kafan either.

The shroud can either be laid out in the coffin, on the floor or on a table, wherever it is easiest at the moment. Many cities/towns now have provision to bury the body without a casket, however for transportation it is still placed inside a temporary casket. Once the shroud has been put on, the body can then be put inside the casket if needed.

- Once the body has been dried, wrap the covering sheet around the body so when it is moved it does not become exposed.
- Once wrapped, move the body and lay it on top of the shroud ensuring it does not become uncovered.
- Carefully move the Qamīs (shirt) from behind the head and over it so it now covers the body.
- Once the Qamīs has been put on, remove the covering sheet making sure that the body is not exposed.
- Rub some of the camphor mixture onto the places of the body which touched the ground during Sajdah, the forehead, nose, both palms, knees and bottom of the forefeet.

- If it is a female, then part her hair in two from the middle and place one part on either side at the front. So there will be one part on the right shoulder and one part on the left shoulder.
- If it is a female, now put on her Orhni -Scarf around her hair and head. Do not fasten it but tuck it in.
- The next sheet is the Izār or lower cloth. Fold the left side first and tuck it over the Qamīs, then fold the right-hand side over.
- It if is a female, then wrap the Sina'band, the chest cloth in the same way, first fold the left side and then the right.
- The final sheet is now the Lifāfah, again wrap the left side first and then the right.
- The 3 binding strips at the bottom can now be used to tighten the shroud. Do not make them so tight that they can't be opened as the knots will need to be opened again.

Visiting the deceased before the Burial.

Once the body has been shrouded, there is normally a short while before the burial takes place. The usual custom is to take the body of the deceased back to the house or leave them in another area where people can come to pay their respects. We must take great care that we do not laugh and joke, talk about worldly affairs etc. when we are in the presence of the deceased.

Question: Who is allowed to see the body of the deceased?

Answer: We must take great care in ensuring only the people who are allowed by Sharī'ah can view the body of the deceased. If the deceased is female, then only members who were her mahram during her life time are allowed to see her body. Any males who are not maḥram should not be allowed to view the body. If the deceased is a male, then again only females from his family should be allowed to view him.

There may be instances where the family do not wish for the face to be uncovered. We must respect their wishes and not demand that we see it.

Question: How should the body be carried?

Answer: There is a Ḥadīth in Jāmiʿ al-Tirmidhī where Abū Hurayrah ﴿رَضِيَ ٱللَّهُ عَنْهُ﴾ narrates that he heard Rasūlullāh ﷺ say "Whoever follows a Janāzah and carries it 3 times then indeed he has fulfilled its rights over him."

أَبَا الْمُهَزِّم قَالَ صَحِبْتُ أَبَا هُرَيْرَةَ عَشْرَ سِنِينَ سَمِعْتُهُ يَقُولُ سَمِعْتُ رَسُولَ اللَّهِ صَلَّى اللَّهُ عَلَيْهِ وَسَلَّمَ يَقُولُ مَنْ تَبِعَ جَنَازَةً وَحَمَلَهَا ثَلَاثَ مَرَّاتٍ فَقَدْ قَضَى مَا عَلَيْهِ مِنْ حَقِّهَا[21]

The above Ḥadīth has been classified as weak due to the narrator Abul Muhazzim.

There is no specific way in which the Janāzah should be carried. As long as the body is carried carefully and swiftly as per the Ḥadīth below.

---

[21] Jāmiʿ al-Tirmidhī 962

عَنْ أَبِي هُرَيْرَةَ يَبْلُغُ بِهِ النَّبِيَّ صَلَّى اللَّهُ عَلَيْهِ وَسَلَّمَ قَالَ أَسْرِعُوا بِالْجَنَازَةِ فَإِنْ يَكُنْ خَيْرًا تُقَدِّمُوهَا إِلَيْهِ وَإِنْ يَكُنْ شَرًّا تَضَعُوهُ عَنْ رِقَابِكُمْ²²

Abu Hurayrah ؓ narrates that the Prophet ﷺ said "Walk swiftly with the Janāzah, if the deceased is a good person then you are sending them towards good and if he is a bad person then you are putting down the bad from your shoulders."

Each person if possible, should try and help carry the body of the deceased. Care must be taken if it's the Janāzah of a female and is being carried without a casket, just in the shroud. Only her maḥrams should carry her. If the deceased is a child, then it should be carried by one person at a time.

Question: What should we pray when we are sat neat the body?

Answer: We should read the Qur'ān, especially Sūrah Yāsīn. We can busy ourselves in any dhikr and also perform Du'ā for oneself and for the deceased. Do not engage in worldly talk.

Question: Does crying cause the deceased person punishment?

Answer: If the dead person has left a bequest for women to come and mourn for him then this will be a means of punishment for the deceased. Natural crying does not cause punishment for

---

²² Jāmi' al-Tirmidhī 936

the deceased however we must refrain from overdoing it or crying on purpose when we visit the house or family of the deceased.

THE JANĀZAH PRAYER

Once the Ghusl has been completed, the body is ready for the Janāzah Prayer. The Janāzah Prayer is not only performed for the forgiveness of the deceased, but also out of respect for the deceased. In the same way the Janāzah prayer is also performed for innocent children.

The Janāzah Prayer is Farḍ Kifāyah. This means that from the locality at least one person should attend, and the obligation will be fulfilled on behalf of the whole community, however if no one attends, then all will be sinful.

To attend the Janāzah, is also one of the rights of a Muslim as shown in the Ḥadith below:

عَنْ أَبَا هُرَيْرَةَ رضى الله عنه قَالَ سَمِعْتُ رَسُولَ اللَّهِ صلى الله

عليه وسلم يَقُولُ

حَقُّ الْمُسْلِمِ عَلَى الْمُسْلِمِ خَمْسٌ رَدُّ السَّلاَمِ وَعِيَادَةُ الْمَرِيضِ

وَاتِّبَاعُ الْجَنَائِزِ وَإِجَابَةُ الدَّعْوَةِ وَتَشْمِيتُ الْعَاطِسِ [23]

Abū Hurayrah ﷺ mentions that I heard Rasūlullāh ﷺ saying, "The rights of a Muslim on the Muslims are five: to respond to the Salām, visiting the sick, to follow the funeral processions, to accept an invitation, and to reply to those who sneeze"

---

[23] Ṣaḥīḥ al-Bukhārī 1240

For the person reading the prayer, there is great reward.

عَنْ أَبِي هُرَيْرَةَ قَالَ قَالَ رَسُولُ اللَّهِ صَلَّى اللَّهُ عَلَيْهِ وَسَلَّمَ مَنْ صَلَّى عَلَى جَنَازَةٍ فَلَهُ قِيرَاطٌ وَمَنْ تَبِعَهَا حَتَّى يُقْضَى دَفْنُهَا فَلَهُ قِيرَاطَانِ أَحَدُهُمَا أَوْ أَصْغَرُهُمَا مِثْلُ أُحُدٍ[24]

Abū Hurayrah ﷺ narrated that the Prophet ﷺ said "The person who reads the Janāzah Prayer will get the reward of one Qirāṭ and the one who follows the Janāzah until its burial has finished for him there are 2 Qirāṭs, one of them or the smaller of them is equivalent to Uḥud".

It is important not to rush the Janāzah Ṣalāh and allow sufficient time for the people to supplicate for the deceased.

عَنْ أَبِى هُرَيْرَةَ قَالَ سَمِعْتُ رَسُولَ اللَّهِ صلى الله عليه وسلم يَقُولُ " إِذَا صَلَّيْتُمْ عَلَى الْمَيِّتِ فَأَخْلِصُوا لَهُ الدُّعَاءَ "[25]

Rasūlullāh ﷺ said
"When you perform Salāh for the deceased, supplicate sincerely for him"

---

[24] Jāmiʿ al-Tirmidhī 961

[25] Sunan Ibn Mājah 1497

The location of the Janāzah Ṣalāh could vary. It is normally performed at the Cemetery just prior to the burial however there are instances where the Janāzah Prayer is carried out after a prescribed prayer in the Masjid Car Park.

There are also instances where the body is left outside the Masjid and the prayer is done inside the Masjid if there are adverse weather conditions. The Janāzah Ṣalāh is allowed in the Masājid under other extreme conditions like curfews, or permission is not granted to read the Ṣalāh outside or in the Cemetery.

Question:　Is it better for the Imām of the local Masjid to lead Janāzah Ṣalāh or the walī such as the son or father?

Answer:　The default position is that it is better for the Imām of the local Masjid to lead the Janāzah Ṣalāh, followed by the father and then the son. However, if the walī such as the father or the son is more learned than the Imām, it is preferred that they lead Ṣalāh. This has been mentioned by many later Ḥanafī jurists. This however is not necessary, it is the right of the walī to decide who will lead the Ṣalāh.[26]

Question:　Sometimes when we read the Janāzah Ṣalāh, the floor is wet or muddy, can we read the Janāzah Ṣalāh with our shoes on?

Answer:　This question has been answered by Maulānā Ashraf Ali Thanvi رَحِمَهُ اللّٰه. For those people who wish to pray with their

---

[26] https://islamicportal.co.uk/should-the-imam-of-the-local-masjid-lead-janazah-salah-or-the-wali/

shoes on, it is necessary that the spot on which they are standing is pure, and that their shoes are also pure. If they remove their shoes and stand on them, then it is necessary that only the shoes be pure. If people are not mindful of this, then their Ṣalāh will not be valid.[27]

Question: What is the ruling on performing Janāzah Ṣalāh upon a person who deliberately commits suicide and kills himself?

Answer: Suicide is not permitted in Islām. However, Janāzah Ṣalāh and other burial arrangements will be made as normal.

It should be noted that in most cases of suicide, there are underlying psychological and medical factors that lead to this. People should avoid making any judgments and leave the matter to Almighty Allāh. It is also worth noting that in some cases, it is difficult to decide with certainty whether the person deliberately decided to kill themselves or whether the intention was self-harm.[28]

Question: Is there any basis in the Ḥadīths for giving advice in the graveyard during burial?

Answer: Giving advice and teaching people is generally recommended and there are Ḥadīths which clearly mention that Rasūlullāh ﷺ gave advice to the Companions in the graveyard

---

[27] Heavenly Ornaments P255

[28] https://islamicportal.co.uk/janazah-salah-for-one-who-commits-suicide/

during a burial. However, this is not a specific Sunnah of the burial and therefore should avoid becoming a regular occurrence at every burial. It should also not result in any delays in the Janāzah Ṣalāh or the burial.[29]

How should the Janāzah Ṣalāh be read?

The Janāzah Ṣalāh is read in a standing position, there will be no Rukūʿ, Sajdah or sitting. Depending on the school of thought you follow, there will be a slight variance in what will be recited within the Ṣalāh. There will be four Takbīrs in total.

The Body will be placed at the head of the congregation. As per normal Ṣalāh, everyone will be facing in the direction of Qiblah.

The Imām will try and organize the congregation into an odd number of lines. If there is a small congregation then a minimum of three lines should be formed.

قَالَ رَسُولُ اللَّهِ صَلَّى اللَّهُ عَلَيْهِ وَسَلَّمَ مَنْ صَلَّى عَلَيْهِ ثَلَاثَةُ صُفُوفٍ فَقَدْ أَوْجَبَ [30]

---

[29] https://islamicportal.co.uk/giving-advice-in-graveyard-during-burial/

[30] Jāmiʿ al-Tirmidhī 949

Rasūlullāh ﷺ said

"Whosoever has the Ṣalāh of Janāzah prayed on him in 3 lines, Jannat will be Wājib upon him"

The meaning of this Ḥadīth is that the person who's Ṣalāh of Janāzah has a large congregation, they will be forgiven.

Note: We must not raise the level of forming an odd number of rows up to an obligatory Status (Wujūb). If possible then do so but if it is a large congregation and it becomes difficult then there is no harm in having either an odd or even number of rows.

Note: It is Makrūh (undesirable) to read the Janāzah Ṣalāh at Sunrise, Mid-noon (Zawāl) and Sunset. However if the Janāzah arrives at that time then it will be permissible to read the Ṣalāh. If the Janāzah had arrived before the Makrūh time and the Ṣalāh was delayed until that time, then it will be Makrūh. It would be better to wait until after the Makrūh time has elapsed.

Question: Where will the Imām stand in the Janāzah Ṣalāh?

Answer: There is a difference of opinion as to where the Imām will stand however these differences are only on which is the most preferred method. The Imām will stand level with the chest of the deceased, however for a female, this will only be done if the body has been covered properly. If it has not, then the Imām should stand level with the abdomen.

If the congregation is large, then a few people should be nominated to repeat the Takbīrs of the Imām so the whole congregation can hear.

The Imām will read the first Takbīr and fold his hands. The congregation will also do the same.

According to Imām Abū Ḥanīfah رَحِمَهُ اللهُ and Imām Mālik رَحِمَهُ اللهُ, Thanā' will be read. According to Imām Shāfiʿī رَحِمَهُ اللهُ and Imām Aḥmad ibn Ḥambal رَحِمَهُ اللهُ, Sūrah Fātiḥah will be read.

The Thanā' is as follows:

$$\text{سُبْحَانَكَ اللّٰهُمَّ وَ بِحَمْدِكَ وَتَبَارَكَ اسْمُكَ وَ تَعَالىٰ جَدُّك وَلاَ اِله غَيْرُكَ}$$

Note: In many books of jurisprudence & supplications, the additional words, "Wa Jalla Thanā'uka" are mentioned as part of the Thanā'. No Ḥadīth was found stating that those words were also read specifically for the Thanā' in Janāzah Ṣalāh. Therefore it would advisable to read the normal Thanā' which is read in all the other Ṣalāh.[31]

The Imām will then read the second Takbīr loudly, the congregation will also read the Takbīr but quietly. No one will raise their hands to their ears when they recite the Takbīr.

---

[31] https://islamicportal.co.uk/five-questions-regarding-janazah-salah-and-burial/

After the second Takbīr, recite Durūd Sharīf. The best Durūd to read is Durūd Ibrāhīm as shown below.

اَللَّهُمَّ صَلِّ عَلَى مُحَمَّدٍ وَ عَلَى اَلِ مُحَمَّدٍ كَمَا صَلَّيْتَ عَلَى إِبْرَاهِيْمَ وَ عَلَى اَلِ إِبْرَاهِيْمَ اِنَّكَ حَمِيْدٌ مَّجِيْدٌ.اَللّٰهُمَّ بَارِكْ عَلَى مُحَمَّدٍ وَ عَلَى اَلِ مُحَمَّدٍ كَمَا بَارَكْتَ عَلَى إِبْرَاهِيْمَ وَ عَلَى اَلِ إِبْرَاهِيْمَ اِنَّكَ حَمِيْدٌ مَّجِيْدٌ.

The Imām will then read the 3ʳᵈ Takbīr loudly. The congregation will also read the Takbīr but quietly. Again no one will lift their hands to their ears when reciting the Takbīr.

After the 3ʳᵈ Takbīr, there are various Ḥadīth as to which Duʿā was prayed by the Prophet ﷺ [32]. Any of these Duʿā's can be read, we just have to make sure that we invoke forgiveness for the deceased in the Duʿā. In a Ḥadīth narrated by Abū Hurayrah ؓ the following Duʿā was recited

اَللَّهُمَّ اغْفِرْ لِحَيِّنَا وَ مَيِّتِنَا وَ شَاهِدِنَا وَ غَائِبِنَا وَ صَغِيْرِنَا وَ كَبِيْرِنَا وَ ذَكَرِنَا وَ اُنْثَانَا اَللَّهُمَّ مَنْ اَحْيَيْتَهُ مِنَّا فَاَحْيِهِ عَلَى الْإِسْلَامِ وَ مَنْ تَوَفَّيْتَ هُ مِنَّا فَتَوَفَّهُ عَلَى اِلاِيْمَانِ [33]

---

[32] https://islamicportal.co.uk/janazah-salah-duas/

[33] Jāmiʿ al-Tirmidhī 945

The meaning of the above Duʿā is "Oh Allāh forgive the people who are living and those who are dead, the ones who are present and the ones who are absent, the young from amongst us and the old from amongst us, the males and the females. Oh Allāh, the one who you wish to keep alive from us, make him live according to Islām, and the one whom you wish to die from amongst us, make him die on Īmān".

The Imām will then read the 4th and final Takbīr. The congregation will follow again, reading it quietly and no one raising their hands.

The Imām will conclude the Ṣalāh by reciting Salāms twice.

Janāzah Salāh for a Child

The Janāzah Prayer will be read on all children who have been born alive. If any child has been still born, then they will be wrapped in a clean sheet and buried without the Janāzah Prayer.

The method of the Janāzah prayer will be exactly the same as an adult however the Duʿā recited after the 3rd Takbīr may be different. Again any Duʿā which has been narrated can be read. Our Ḥanafī jurists have mentioned that if the deceased is a minor, those supplications should not be read which specifically requests for forgiveness for the deceased person because the minor has no sins.

Maulānā Yusuf Shabbir has addressed this subject in 3 different articles on the islamicportal.co.uk web site. It would be preferable to read the following two supplications along with the normal supplication which is read during the Janāzah Ṣalah of adults mentioned in the previous section.

$$\text{اَللَّهُمَّ اجْعَلْهُ لَنَا فَرَطًا وَسَلَفًا وَأَجْرًا}$$

$$\text{اَاللَّهُمَّ أَعِذْهُ مِنْ عَذَابِ الْقَبْرِ}$$

Moving the body to the Cemetery

There are many burials taking place each day so arrive at the Cemetery beforehand to avoid delays. Ensure you take traffic and distance into account when you are leaving for the Cemetery.

The body should be put in a suitable vehicle to allow transportation to the Cemetery. The local burial committee may have an appropriate vehicle, if not arrange a suitable vehicle. Do not spend excessive amounts in hiring hearses to transport the body and the family to go to the Cemetery.

Once the body arrives at the Cemetery, preparations should be made for the Janāzah Ṣalāt, if it hasn't been read. Please refer to the previous section for the procedure on how to read the Janāzah Ṣalāh.

The Undertaker may need a copy of the registration form (Certificate of Burial) in order to give permission to proceed with the burial. Once permission has been granted, the burial can proceed.

THE ISLAMIC BURIAL PROCESS

Items needed for burial:

- Spades for filling in grave
- Wooden Planks cut to size if body is being buried without Casket
- Unbaked Bricks if necessary
- Large Covering Sheet if female

The grave will have already been dug. Depending on the cemetery and the arrangement with the local authority, the graves will be dug differently. The main two types of graves are Shaq (ditch) and Laḥd (niche). In this country, due to the soft ground we use the Shaq type of grave.

Question:	It is customary whenever a Janāzah is lifted and people transfer it shoulder to shoulder to recite the Shahādah or some other form of dhikr loudly. Is there any basis for this in the Sunnah?
Answer:	The remembrance of Allāh سُبْحَانَهُ وَتَعَالَى is recommended at all times. However, we have not come any basis for saying the Shahādah or Kalimah loudly when lifting and transferring the deceased. The jurists generally discourage loud dhikr when handling the deceased and suggest that a person should engage in the remembrance of Allāh quietly.[34]

---

[34] https://islamicportal.co.uk/loud-dhikr-and-shahadah-when-lifting-and-transferring-the-deceased/

Question: Should we walk in front of the Janāzah or behind it?

Answer: According to the Jurists, it is permissible to walk in front of the Janāzah, behind it, or to the side, the only difference of opinion is in what is most Afḍal (preferential). According to the Hanafi School of thought, it is better to walk behind the Janāzah.

We must ensure that the close family are around the grave, especially if the deceased is a female.

Laying the body in the Grave

The body should be carried to the grave and placed on the side of the grave towards Qiblah. The grave will have been dug so the right-hand side of it will be facing Qiblah.

Once the body has been laid on the side of the grave, depending on the size of the deceased, a few people should lower themselves in the grave; if it is a woman then it should be her maḥrams only.

Note: We must ensure that there are not lots of people shouting out instructions at this point, it should only be the people who know what needs to be done.

Before the people lower themselves inside the grave, it must be explained to them what needs to be done with the body of the deceased, rather than instruct them whilst they are inside the grave. This would best be done by a local scholar.

Note: When the body is being lowered into the grave, the Ḥadīth below informs us of what Duʿā should be prayed.

عَنْ ابْنِ عُمَرَ قَالَ كَانَ النَّبِيُّ صَلَّى اللَّهُ عَلَيْهِ وَسَلَّمَ إِذَا أُدْخِلَ الْمَيِّتُ الْقَبْرَ قَالَ بِسْمِ اللَّهِ وَعَلَى مِلَّةِ رَسُولِ اللَّهِ [35]

Ibn Umar ﷺ narrates that the Prophet ﷺ, whenever he would put the deceased in the grave, he would say:

بِسْمِ اللَّهِ وَعَلَى مِلَّةِ رَسُولِ اللَّهِ

Note: If it is a female, then a sheet should be used to cover the grave while her body is being lowered into the grave. The sheet should be held by her maḥrams as well if possible. In the situation where there are not enough, then close family members should hold the sheet. Any males that are not maḥram should move back whilst the body is being laid inside the grave. Once the body is covered by the bricks, wooden planks, the casket cover or soil, it will be ok for them to return to help fill the grave.

The procedure will be that the body of the deceased will be passed to them while they are inside the grave. They will slowly lower the body into the grave and place it on the right-hand side close to the Qiblah.

Once the body has been laid down, if it is inside the coffin then the casket will be opened and the body will be shifted to the right-hand side of the coffin, as

---

[35] Sunan Ibn Mājah 1539

close to the Qiblah as possible. Pieces of earth will then be used to tilt the body towards Qiblah. If the body is not in a casket, as mentioned before, it should also be moved to the right-hand side as close to the Qiblah as possible.

Note: The whole body should be turned towards the Qiblah and not just the head in a manner similar to the Sunnah method of sleeping as per the diagram below.[36]

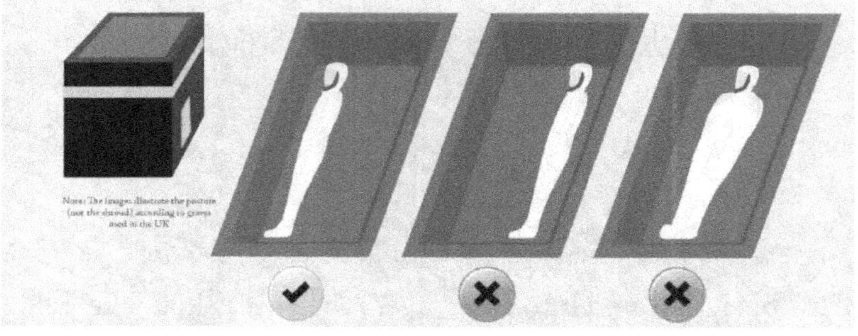

Once the body has been laid and turned, if it is inside a coffin, the knots should all be untied, and the casket closed. If the body is not in a casket and is in a Laḥd or Shaq grave, the knots should be untied then the planks of wood or bricks should be laid.

Note: Once the body has been moved to face the Qiblah, no more than 2 people are needed inside the grave for the next stage. Any extra people should come out of the grave carefully.

---

[36] https://islamicportal.co.uk/the-correct-method-of-burying-the-deceased/

If the burial is being done without a casket, then starting from the head side for a female or the feet side for a male, lay the bricks or planks of wood close to each other ensuring there is no gap.

If the grave is a standard rectangular grave then the planks of wood should be wedged in at 45 degrees like the diagram shown on the following page (this would be for a male, for a female as mentioned, you would start from the head side).

Filling the Grave

Once all of the wood or bricks have been laid, large clumps of earth should be manually laid on the floor of the grave. These should be passed to the people inside the grave so they can place them carefully. Do not throw in large clumps of mud from the outside.

The people inside the grave should now come out. The grave should then be filled in a timely manner, not rushing it or doing it in a way by which the wood or bricks become dislodged. This could be a difficult task so as many people as possible should try and get involved.

Supplications during burial

It is desirable to throw in 3 handfuls of dirt into the grave. The Ḥadīth below from Dār Quṭnī, mentions that 3 handfuls of dirt were thrown by the Prophet ﷺ whilst he was standing near the head of the body. If a person is able to do it easily then there is no issue, but people should not be forced into doing this as sometimes is the case.

عن عبد الله بن عامر بن ربيعة عن أبيه قال : رأيت النبى صلى الله عليه و سلم حين دفن عثمان بن مظعون صلى عليه وكبر عليه أربعا وحثى على قبره بيده ثلاث حثيات من التراب وهو قائم عند رأس [37]

It is also Mustaḥab to read the supplication below during the burial.

مِنْهَا خَلَقْنَاكُمْ وَفِيهَا نُعِيدُكُمْ وَمِنْهَا نُخْرِجُكُمْ تَارَةً أُخْرَى

"From the earth We created you, and We shall return you to it, and from it We shall raise you once again"

Some scholars have further mentioned that it is desirable to take three handful of soil and split the three parts of the verse on each handful

---

[37] Sunan Dār Quṭnī Volume 2 – Page 76

respectively, However, we have not come across any Ḥadīth to substantiate this.[38]

The Ḥadīth below shows the basis for the recitation of this Duʿā. Although the narration has been classified as weak, Imām Nawawī رحمه الله (d. 676/1277) and others have deemed it acceptable to act upon this narration

عَنْ أَبِى أُمَامَةَ قَالَ لَمَّا وُضِعَتْ أُمُّ كُلْثُومٍ ابْنَةُ رَسُولِ اللَّهِ صَلَّى اللَّهُ عَلَيْهِ وَسَلَّمَ فِي الْقَبْرِ قَالَ رَسُولُ اللَّهِ صَلَّى اللَّهُ عَلَيْهِ وَسَلَّمَ

{ مِنْهَا خَلَقْنَاكُمْ وَفِيهَا نُعِيدُكُمْ وَمِنْهَا نُخْرِجُكُمْ تَارَةً أُخْرَى }[39]

Abī Umāmah رضي الله عنه narrates that when Umme Kulthūm رضي الله عنها the daughter of the Prophet صلى الله عليه وسلم was put into her grave, the Prophet صلى الله عليه وسلم said "From the earth We created you, and We shall return you to it, and from it We shall raise you once again"

How high to raise the Grave?

When filling the grave, ensure that it is not raised too high. It should be filled to a level where people can recognize that it is a grave, so they don't walk over it, sit on it, throw their rubbish on it etc.

---

[38] https://islamicportal.co.uk/five-questions-regarding-janazah-salah-and-burial/

[39] Sunan Imam Aḥmad 21163

It should be shaped like a camel's hump, like mentioned in the Ḥadīth below:

$$\text{عَنْ سُفْيَانَ التَّمَّارِ أَنَّهُ حَدَّثَهُ}$$

$$\text{أَنَّهُ رَأَى قَبْرَ النَّبِيِّ صَلَّى اللَّهُ عَلَيْهِ وَسَلَّمَ مُسَنَّمًا}^{40}$$

Sufyān Tammār ﷺ narrates that he saw the Grave of the Prophet ﷺ and it was shaped like a hump.

Sprinkling Water on the Grave

Once the grave has been filled, water can be sprinkled onto the grave.

$$\text{ابن عمر عن أبيه أن رسول الله صلى الله عليه وسلم رش على}$$

$$\text{قبر ابنه إبراهيم}^{41}$$

Ibn ʿUmar ﷺ narrates "The Prophet ﷺ sprinkled water on the grave of his son Ibrāhīm".

There is further clarification on the actual procedure in the Ḥadīth below.

---

[40] Ṣaḥīḥ al-Bukhārī 1302

[41] Abū Dāwūd – Marāsīl 399

جابر بن عبد الله قال رش على قبر النبي صلى الله عليه و سلم

الماء رشا قال وكان الذي رش الماء على قبره بلال بن رباح بقربة

بدأ من قبل رأسه من شقه الأيمن حتى انتهى إلى رجليه [42]

Jābir ؓ narrates that water was sprinkled on the grave of our Prophet ﷺ and the one who sprinkled water on the grave was Bilāl ibn Rabāḥ with a water skin. He started from the side of the head towards the right and finished towards the feet.

The wisdom behind sprinkling the water is to help settle the grave as mentioned in Durre-Mukhtār

Planting a Branch at the Head of the Grave

Another action which is very common is that a branch is taken off a tree and planted at the head of the grave. The basis for this action is taken from the Ḥadīth below.

عَنْ ابْنِ عَبَّاسٍ قَالَ مَرَّ النَّبِيُّ صَلَّى اللَّهُ عَلَيْهِ وَسَلَّمَ بِقَبْرَيْنِ فَقَالَ

إِنَّهُمَا لَيُعَذَّبَانِ وَمَا يُعَذَّبَانِ فِي كَبِيرٍ أَمَّا أَحَدُهُمَا فَكَانَ لَا يَسْتَتِرُ مِنْ

الْبَوْلِ وَأَمَّا الْآخَرُ فَكَانَ يَمْشِي بِالنَّمِيمَةِ ثُمَّ أَخَذَ جَرِيدَةً رَطْبَةً

---

[42] Sunan al-Bayhaqī al-Kubrā' 6534

فَشَقَّهَا نِصْفَيْنِ فَغَرَزَ فِي كُلِّ قَبْرٍ وَاحِدَةً قَالُوا يَا رَسُولَ اللهِ لِمَ فَعَلْتَ هَذَا قَالَ لَعَلَّهُ يُخَفِّفُ عَنْهُمَا مَا لَمْ يَيْبَسَا[43]

Ibn Abbās ﷺ narrates that the Prophet ﷺ passed by two graves and he said "Indeed both of them are being punished and they are not being punished for a great thing. As for one of them, he didn't save himself from being soiled with his urine and as for the other, he used to walk around causing enmity between friends". Then the Prophet ﷺ took a fresh palm leaf and split it in half and planted one on each grave. He was asked why you did this, he said "I hope that their torture might be lessened, till these get dried"

The preferred view is that this action is permissible if a person wishes to do so. However, it should not be made habitual as it is only narrated once from the Prophetic era, and once or twice thereafter from the practice of the companions.

Note: Nowadays people cause more harm to the trees in the Cemetery attempting to pull down branches. We must take great care in not causing damage to the Cemetery itself and the trees.

---

[43] Ṣaḥīḥ al-Bukhāri 211

Reading Opening & Closing Verses of Surah Al-Baqarah after burial

Once the grave has been filled, the usual practise is to read the first Rukūʿ of Sūrah al-Baqarah near the head of the grave and the last Rukūʿ of Sūrah al-Baqarah near the foot of the grave. The Ḥadīth below shows that the reference Ḥadīth for this action is Mawqūf (suspended) on Ibn ʿUmar ﷺ.

عبد الله بن عمر سمعت النبي صلى الله عليه و سلم يقول

إذا مات أحدكم فلا تحبسوه و أسرعوا به إلى قبره و ليقرأ عند

رأسه فاتحة الكتاب و عند رجليه بخاتمة البقرة فى قبره

لم يكتب إلا بهذا الإسناد فيما أعلم و قد روينا القراءة

المذكورة فيه عن ابن عمر موقوفا عليه ⁴⁴

There is another narration by Imām Tabarāni ﷺ where Rasūlullāh ﷺ is reported to have recited the opening verses and final verses of [Sūrah] al-Baqarah by his head.

Many jurists have considered the aforementioned narrations and recommended that the opening five verses of Sūrah al-Baqarah should be recited by the head and the final two verses should be read by the feet. Others

---

44 Shuʿ'bal Imān – al-Bayhaqī 9294

have suggested that the opening and final verses of Sūrah al-Baqarah should be recited by the head. There is therefore flexibility in this matter. Similarly, it is permissible to recite Sūrah al-Fātiḥah instead of the first five verses of Sūrah al-Baqarah.[45]

Appendix D contains the opening and closing verses of Sūrah Al-Baqarah.

Supplicating for the Deceased

After this, it is advisable to stay a while and supplicate for the deceased whilst facing the Qiblah as mentioned in the Ḥadīth Below.

عُثْمَانَ بْنِ عَفَّانَ قَالَ كَانَ النَّبِيُّ صَلَّى اللَّهُ عَلَيْهِ وَسَلَّمَ إِذَا فَرَغَ مِنْ دَفْنِ الْمَيِّتِ وَقَفَ عَلَيْهِ فَقَالَ اسْتَغْفِرُوا لِأَخِيكُمْ وَسَلُوا لَهُ بِالتَّثْبِيتِ فَإِنَّهُ الْآنَ يُسْأَلُ[46]

ʿUthmān ibn ʿAffān ﷺ narrates that when the Prophet ﷺ used to finish burying the deceased he would stand over him and say
"Seek forgiveness for your brother and ask steadfastness for him, for indeed he is being questioned now".

---

[45] https://islamicportal.co.uk/five-questions-regarding-janazah-salah-and-burial/#_ftn16

[46] Sunan Abū Dāwūd 2804

Question: Should the hands be raised when supplicating after the burial?

Answer: There is no harm in raising the hands whilst making Duʿā so as long as it is not regarded necessary and one faces the Qiblah.[47]

Note: We have not come across any Ḥadīth that suggests that Rasūlullāh ﷺ would make congregational Duʿā after burial in the way that has become customary in our community. If however a congregational Duʿā takes place, this is permissible on the condition that the congregational feature is not regarded as a post-burial Sunnah and it does not become a habitual practice.

It is therefore important to educate the community gradually in a constructive manner and avoid using the prevalent congregational mode habitually.

Finally, it is worth noting that the primary purpose of Janāzah Ṣalāh is supplication and seeking forgiveness for the deceased. Imāms should therefore not rush the Janāzah Ṣalāh

---

[47] https://islamicportal.co.uk/five-questions-regarding-janazah-salah-and-burial/#_ftn16

and allow themselves and the congregation sufficient time after the third Takbīr to make Duʿā.[48]

Preparing Food for the Day of the Funeral

If any people are attending the funeral from far then they should make preparation for food themselves. If for any reason they have not made preparations and there is an excess of food at the household of the deceased, then there is no issue in them eating it, if invited to do so. Visitors cannot make any demands for food or drink.

Organising food for guests who have travelled from a distance is permissible subject to the following conditions:

- The food must not be prepared from the wealth of the deceased or the wealth of minors.
- It should only be intended for guests who have travelled from a distance and the family of the deceased along with those who are busy assisting with the burial arrangements.
- There should be no Iltizām; it should not be expected or considered necessary.
- It should not become a burden on the family of the deceased or anyone else.
- It should not take the form of a daʿwat to which people are invited, rather, whoever happens to be present, can eat from the food. This

---

[48] https://islamicportal.co.uk/five-questions-regarding-janazah-salah-and-burial/#_ftn16

includes those from the locality who are assisting with the funeral arrangements as mentioned above.

Ideally, the people in the locality should make arrangements for such guests. However, it is also permissible for the family or the associates of the deceased to make such arrangements.[49]

---

[49] https://islamicportal.co.uk/feeding-the-family-of-the-deceased-and-others/

BUILDING STRUCTURES OF GRAVES

عَنْ جَابِرٍ قَالَ نَهَى النَّبِيُّ صَلَّى اللَّهُ عَلَيْهِ وَسَلَّمَ أَنْ تُجَصَّصَ الْقُبُورُ وَأَنْ يُكْتَبَ عَلَيْهَا وَأَنْ يُبْنَى عَلَيْهَا وَأَنْ تُوطَأَ [50]

"Jabir ؓ narrates that the Prophet ﷺ told us not to make our graves built up, not to write on them, not to build on them and not to walk on them"

From this Ḥadīth we can see that graves should not be made into structures. We should not write any excessive words on the grave stones, especially verses from the Qur'ān and we should not spend excessive amounts decorating the graves.

Graves maybe used over and over again, so if they have large gravestones and built up structures, they will be difficult to remove and prevent others from also getting buried there. If we look at the example of the cemeteries in Makkah and Madīnah, they have the capability of burying thousands of people in the same cemeteries again and again. This would not be possible if all of the graves were built up.

Note: There is no harm in having a small gravestone and writing the name of the deceased on it to identify the plot of the deceased and prevent it from

---

[50] Jāmiʿ al-Tirmidhī 972

being desecrated. A large gravestone will incur a lot more cost, in terms of both the council fees and the cost of the gravestone itself. This extra money would be better spent towards a charitable cause which will benefit the deceased.

The gravestone should be kept as simple as possible and placed at the head of the grave. The gravestone should not cover the whole grave and have extra stones and pebbles on it for ornamental value.

VISITING THE CEMETERY

The purpose of visiting a Cemetery is two-fold. It is a reminder for us that our lives in this world are temporary and our visit is also beneficial to the deceased.

عَنِ ابْنِ مَسْعُودٍ أَنَّ رَسُولَ اللَّهِ صلى الله عليه وسلم

قَالَ كُنْتُ نَهَيْتُكُمْ عَنْ زِيَارَةِ الْقُبُورِ فَزُورُوا الْقُبُورَ فَإِنَّهَا تُزَهِّدُ

فِي الدُّنْيَا وَتُذَكِّرُ الآخِرَةَ[51]

Ibn Masʿūd ؓ narrates that Rasūlullāh ﷺ said
"I used to forbid you to visit the graves, but now visit them, for they will draw your attention away from this world and remind you of the Hereafter."

When visiting the Cemetery be respectful at all times, do not laugh and joke. It is a time for reflection and introspection, as we could be the next person to be buried. The thought should be, have we prepared enough if we were to pass away now?

When entering the Cemetery, there are various Duʿās mentioned in the Aḥādīth which we can recite. We must face the graves and greet them, then supplicate for ourselves and the deceased. People tend to forget to do Duʿā for themselves as well at this point.

---

[51] Sunan Ibn Mājah 1571

The Duʿā below has been mentioned in a Ḥadith in Ṣaḥīḥ Muslim

السَّلَامُ عَلَيْكُمْ أَهْلَ الدِّيَارِ مِنَ الْمُؤْمِنِينَ وَالْمُسْلِمِينَ وَإِنَّا إِنْ شَاءَ اللَّهُ لَلَاحِقُونَ أَسْأَلُ اللَّهَ لَنَا وَلَكُمُ الْعَافِيَةَ[52]

"Peace be upon you, dwellers of the grave, among the believers, and Muslims, and indeed God willing we shall join you. I seek well-being from Allāh, for you and us"

The Duʿā below has been mentioned in a Ḥadīth in Jāmiʿ al-Tirmidhī.

السَّلَامُ عَلَيْكُمْ يَا أَهْلَ الْقُبُورِ يَغْفِرُ اللَّهُ لَنَا وَلَكُمْ أَنْتُمْ سَلَفُنَا وَنَحْنُ بِالْأَثَرِ[53]

"Oh dwellers of the grave! Peace be upon you, may Allāh forgive me and you, you are our predecessors and we are coming behind you"

Thereafter busy yourself in praying and supplicating. A person can read Sūrah Yāsīn as well as other Duʿās and Sūrahs to send as Īsāl al-Thawāb for the deceased. Imagine how much reward you can send forward for the deceased if you spent the duration of your visit busy in the above.

---

[52] Ṣaḥīḥ Muslim 975

[53] Jāmiʿ al-Tirmidhī 973

Remember to pray for all of the deceased in the Cemetery, not just your friends and relatives.

Question: Are we allowed to place flowers on graves?

Answer: There is no basis for this in the Sunnah or the statements of earlier scholars. This must therefore be avoided. Some people purchase flowers to adorn the grave. Adorning the grave in this manner is unsubstantiated and it is more beneficial for the deceased to give this money in charity.[54]

---

[54] https://islamicportal.co.uk/twigs-and-flowers-on-the-grave/

TAZIYAT – VISTING THE HOUSE OF THE DECEASED

When someone passes away, the people who go for Taziyat (visiting the deceased house to pay respects) or attend the Janāzah should only say good words for the deceased. They should also ask for forgiveness for themselves and for the deceased because at that time the Angels say Amīn to the Duʿās.

A common mistake is that people make Duʿā for the deceased but forget themselves. The Prophet ﷺ taught Umme Salamah رضي الله عنها the method of Duʿā when her husband Abū Salamah رضي الله عنه passed away, in that she was told to do Duʿā for herself first and then for the deceased.

عَنْ أُمِّ سَلَمَةَ قَالَتْ قَالَ لَنَا رَسُولُ اللَّهِ صَلَّى اللَّهُ عَلَيْهِ وَسَلَّمَ إِذَا حَضَرْتُمُ الْمَرِيضَ أَوِ الْمَيِّتَ فَقُولُوا خَيْرًا فَإِنَّ الْمَلَائِكَةَ يُؤَمِّنُونَ عَلَى مَا تَقُولُونَ قَالَتْ فَلَمَّا مَاتَ أَبُو سَلَمَةَ أَتَيْتُ النَّبِيَّ صَلَّى اللَّهُ عَلَيْهِ وَسَلَّمَ فَقُلْتُ يَا رَسُولَ اللَّهِ إِنَّ أَبَا سَلَمَةَ مَاتَ قَالَ فَقُولِي اللَّهُمَّ اغْفِرْ لِي وَلَهُ وَأَعْقِبْنِي مِنْهُ عُقْبَى حَسَنَةً قَالَتْ فَقُلْتُ فَأَعْقَبَنِي اللَّهُ مِنْهُ مَنْ هُوَ خَيْرٌ مِنْهُ رَسُولَ اللَّهِ صَلَّى اللَّهُ عَلَيْهِ وَسَلَّمَ [55]

---

[55] Jāmiʿ al-Tirmidhī 899

Umme Salamah رَضِيَٱللَّهُعَنْهَا says that Rasūlullāh صَلَّىٱللَّهُعَلَيْهِوَسَلَّم said to us whenever you visit the ill or the deceased then say good words, indeed the Angels say Amīn upon what it said. She said, When Abū Salamah رَضِيَٱللَّهُعَنْهُ passed away I went to the Prophet صَلَّىٱللَّهُعَلَيْهِوَسَلَّم and I said, oh Messenger of Allāh صَلَّىٱللَّهُعَلَيْهِوَسَلَّم, Abū Salamah رَضِيَٱللَّهُعَنْهُ has passed away, he said to me, say "Oh Allāh forgive me and forgive him and give me a better return than I got from him". Umme Salamah رَضِيَٱللَّهُعَنْهَا says "When I said these words, Allāh سُبْحَانَهُوَتَعَالَى gave me in return for Abū Salamah رَضِيَٱللَّهُعَنْهُ that person who was better than him - the Messenger of Allāh صَلَّىٱللَّهُعَلَيْهِوَسَلَّم"

We should try and visit the house of the deceased within the three-day mourning period if possible. There is no basis to the custom where upon arrival of new guests, incense sticks are lit, and a group supplication takes place. There is no harm in doing Duʿā but considering it an obligation which every visitor must undertake is incorrect.

The visitors should busy themselves in praying and Duʿā. They should console the members of the household and refrain from asking awkward questions relating to the deceased. We must remember it is a difficult time for them so keep the visit short. One should not make any demands for food and drink when visiting. If the members of the household find more consolation in you spending more time with them, then there is no harm staying for longer.

Preparing Food for the household of the deceased during the mourning period

When the cousin of Rasūlullāh ﷺ, Jaʿfar ؓ passed away, he gave instruction to his household to send food to the household of the deceased.

$$\text{عَبْدِ اللَّهِ بْنِ جَعْفَرٍ قَالَ لَمَّا جَاءَ نَعْيُ جَعْفَرٍ قَالَ النَّبِيُّ صَلَّى اللَّهُ عَلَيْهِ وَسَلَّمَ اصْنَعُوا لِأَهْلِ جَعْفَرٍ طَعَامًا فَإِنَّهُ قَدْ جَاءَهُمْ مَا يَشْغَلُهُمْ}^{56}$$

It is Mustaḥab (desirable) that food is sent to the household of the deceased which is sufficient for one day and one night. This food should be sent by the neighbours or the people close to the household. The reason for this is that during their mourning, the household does not have to worry about preparing food. The person who is sending the food should inform the household so if any other people decide to also cook, they can kindly refuse.

The food should also just be sent, there is no evidence that the people sending the food should sit and partake of the food with the household of the deceased.

There is also no evidence that the food should be sent for more than one day and night, and that food should be prepared for visitors as well. The custom where groups of people get together and take turns in sending food for a

---

[56] Jāmiʿ al-Tirmidhī 919

number of days sharing the cost has no basis. Furthermore inviting people for food after a certain number of days also has no basis.

We have to be very careful that customs which have been passed down through generations are not prioritised in such a way that one believes it to be part of religion. We should not just take these customs on face value as part of our Religion but ask for clear evidence from Qur'ān and Ḥadīth as proof. If in doubt consult the Scholars.

PERIOD OF MOURNING

The mourning period starts immediately after the demise and not the burial. The period of mourning for a woman whose husband has passed away shall be 4 months and 10 days.

For any other relative, the period of mourning shall be 3 days from the moment they passed away. This is to allow the family to try and return to some kind of normality. We should try and visit within these 3 days if possible.

If someone is from outside the city and could not make it within this time, then there is no issue with them visiting the house of the deceased at a later time.

ᶜIddah

By Muftī Ebrahim Desai

Upon the husband's death, or divorce, or the termination of the marriage contract through Khulᶜ (divorce at the instance of the wife), or the annulment of the marriage by some other manner, the woman has to remain staying in one house for a specified period of time. Until this period expires, it is not permissible for her to go elsewhere. The act of passing this period is called ᶜIddah.

If the ᶜIddah, or waiting period, is observed following the death of the husband, it is called 'The ᶜIddah of Death'. If observed following Ṭalāq (divorce), Khul' (divorce at the instance of the wife) or for some other reason, it is called 'The ᶜIddah of divorce'. There are some differences in the rules and periods of the two types of ᶜIddah.

ᶜIddah of Death

Allah سُبْحَانَهُ وَتَعَالَى mentions the ruling of this ᶜIddah in the Holy Qur'ān:

$$وَٱلَّذِينَ يُتَوَفَّوْنَ مِنكُمْ وَيَذَرُونَ اَزْوَاجًا يَتَرَبَّصْنَ بِأَنفُسِهِنَّ اَرْبَعَةَ اَشْهُرٍ وَعَشْرًا^{57}$$

"For those men who die amongst you and leave behind wives,

---

⁵⁷ Sūrah Al-Baqarah 234

they (the wives) must confine themselves (spend ʿIddah) for four months and ten days"

A woman whose husband dies should remain in ʿIddah for four months and ten days. She should live in the house she used to live in at the time of her husband's death. Leaving the home is incorrect.

This rule applies equally whether

1. a woman has had intimacy with her husband during his lifetime or not
2. she had any kind of privacy with him or not
3. she had come to live with him or not
4. she menstruates or not
5. she is old or young
6. she reached the age of puberty or not.

However, if the woman was pregnant at the time of the demise of her husband, she should remain in ʿIddah until the child is born. This applies irrespective of the number of days or months. Even if the child was born just an hour after the husband's death, the ʿIddah will be over.

A woman in ʿIddah may move freely in the house. She does not have to restrict herself to just one room.

If at the time of receiving the news of her husband's demise, a woman was away from the house, for example, to take care of some family chore, or was away visiting neighbours, or visiting her own parents/relatives for a few days (with or without the husband), she should immediately return home. This rule applies irrespective of where the husband passed away, at home or away.

A woman whose displeased husband had sent her to her parental home should, upon her husband's demise, return to the home of her husband and complete her ʿIddah there. As a rule, ʿIddah is completed in the house which was the permanent residence of the wife at the time of her husband's death. Her temporary residence is not taken into consideration. It is obvious that her visit to her parent's home was temporary.

If the husband died on the first of the lunar month and the woman is not pregnant, she will have to complete the period of four months and ten days in accordance with the lunar calendar. And if the husband died on a date other than the first, she would have to complete the period of one hundred and thirty days (four months of thirty days each and ten days) - Maʿārif al-Qurʾān. ʿIddah begins from the time of the husband's death even if the woman is not aware of his death and even though she had made no intention to observe ʿIddah.

If she only received the news of her husband's demise four months and ten days thereafter, her ʿIddah stands completed. She will not have to observe ʿIddah all over again.

If for instance, a woman hears about the death of her husband several days later, but there is uncertainty about the exact date of his death, ʿIddah will be counted from the later date. For example, there is a doubt whether the husband died on the first of November or first of December, the ʿIddah will be counted from the first of December.

ʿIddah of Divorce

When the husband divorces his wife, she will have to spend her ʿIddah in the matrimonial home. She must not leave the house during the day nor at night, nor can she make Nikāḥ with anyone else. Once she completes three Ḥayḍ periods, her ʿIddah will be complete and she can now stay wherever she wishes. This rule will apply irrespective of whether the man issued one two or three divorces, and irrespective of whether he issued a Ṭalāq Bā'in (irrevocable divorce) or a Ṭalāq Rajʿī (revocable Ṭalāq). The same rule will apply in all cases.

The ʿIddah for divorce is only compulsory on the woman who is divorced after her husband had engaged in sexual intercourse with her or, they did not engage in sexual intercourse but they met in privacy and thereafter her husband divorces her. If they did not meet in privacy and the person divorces her, she does not have to observe the ʿIddah.

If a young girl who had not experienced Ḥayḍ, or an old woman whose Ḥayḍ had terminated is divorced, then their ʿIddah will be three months.

A young girl who has not experienced Ḥayḍ as yet was divorced. She therefore commenced her ʿIddah on the basis that it will be three months. However, after a month or two she began experiencing Ḥayḍ. Her ʿIddah will now be calculated from the time her Ḥayḍ commences. She will therefore have to remain in ʿIddah until the completion of three Ḥayḍ periods. Her ʿIddah will not be complete until the completion of three Ḥayḍ periods.

If a woman is pregnant and her husband divorces her, she will have to remain in that house until she delivers her child. When she delivers her child, her

'Iddah will expire even if she delivers her child a few days after being divorced.

If a woman is divorced while she is in her Ḥayḍ, this Ḥayḍ will not be considered. Her 'Iddah will be complete up on the expiry of three Ḥayḍ periods after the Ḥayḍ that she is presently experiencing. However, it should be noted that it is a sin to divorce a woman while she is in her Ḥayḍ.

If she is observing her 'Iddah in the same house wherein the man who issued a Ṭalāq Bā'in to her is also living, she will have to observe strict Pardah with him.

Maintenance During the Period of 'Iddah

The maintenance and providing of shelter for a woman observing the 'Iddah of Death are not the responsibility of her in-laws. She also does not have the right to take her maintenance out of the estate of her deceased husband. However, she will be entitled to her share of Inheritance. The maintenance and providing of shelter for a woman while she is observing her 'Iddah of divorce are Wājib on the very man who divorced her.

'Iddah in the Case of Pregnancy or Miscarriage

As stated earlier, the 'Iddah of a pregnant woman ends with the birth of the child. The ruling however differs in the case of a miscarriage. If any body part of the miscarried foetus was formed, e.g. the mouth, the nose or the fingers, the 'Iddah will end upon the miscarriage. If there was no formation of any limb, the woman will be regarded as not being pregnant, and as a result, her 'Iddah will be four months and ten days.

Rules

The maximum period of pregnancy in the Sharīʿah is two years. Sharīʿah does not recognize pregnancy beyond the period of two years. If a woman was pregnant at the time of her husband's demise, but did not deliver the child within two years thereafter, she would be regarded as not been pregnant. Her ʿIddah had ended four months and ten days after the demise of her husband.

In the case of a multiple conception, e.g. twins, ʿIddah terminates at the birth of the last child.

The Death of the Husband and the ʿIddah of Ṭalāq

If the ʿIddah of Ṭalāq expires and the former husband passes away, there is no ʿIddah of Death. Such a divorcee does not inherit from her former husband's estate.

If the husband passes away before the expiry of the ʿIddah, the ruling will be as follows:

1. If the husband gave his wife a revocable divorce (Ṭalāq Rajʿī) the wife should observe her ʿIddah of Death and she will inherit from his estate.

2. If the husband had given his wife an irrevocable divorce (Ṭalāq Bā'in) while he was in good health, and the husband dies before the expiry of the ʿIddah of Divorce, the woman will complete the ʿIddah of divorce. She will not observe the ʿIddah of Death nor will she inherit from the husband.

3. If the husband, with the consent of the wife, gave her an irrevocable divorce (Ṭalāq Bā'in) during his final illness (Maraḍ al-Mawt) the woman will complete

the remaining period of the ʿIddah of Divorce. She will not observe the ʿIddah of Death nor will she inherit from the husband.

4. If the husband had given his wife an irrevocable divorce (Ṭalāq Bā'in) during his final illness (Maraḍ al-Mawt) without the consent of the wife, then her ʿIddah will be the longer of the two ʿIddahs. She will inherit from the husband's estate.

Things That Are Not Permissible During ʿIddah

A woman observing the ʿIddah of Death should neither go out of the house nor remarry, nor indulge in beautifying herself through make-up. During ʿIddah, all these things are Ḥarām (Forbidden) for her.

Ḥadīth

The Holy Prophet ﷺ has said that it is not permissible for a believer to mourn for anyone for more than three days, except the widow whose period of mourning (when not pregnant) on the death of her husband is four months and ten days.

Observing a Period of Mourning is Wājib

RULES:

- It is necessary (Wājib) upon every adult and sane Muslim woman to observe ʿIddah (mourn) the death of her husband. It is not necessary upon a woman who is a disbeliever, insane or did not attain puberty.

- It is Ḥarām (strictly prohibited) to make an express proposal of marriage to a woman observing the ʿIddah of Death. It is also Ḥarām to contract a Nikāḥ with such a woman. Such a Nikāḥ will be null and void.
- It is Ḥarām upon a female observing ʿIddah to apply perfume; to don ornaments, jewellery or decorations of any sort; to wear eye makeup, such as Kuḥl (antimony) or galena; to chew or apply colour on the lips, teeth or gums; to apply oil on the head; to comb the hair (in order to beautify herself); to use henna; to wear silken or other gaudy dresses.
- It is permissible to bath and wash the hair during ʿIddah.

Using Beauty Aids as Medicine

RULES:

- If there is a need to apply oil to the head because of a headache or lice, only such oil may be used that has no scent.
- If there is a need to use Surmah (antimony) as a balm for the eyes, it will be permissible. In such a case, it should be applied at night and cleared in the morning.
- A female in ʿIddah will be excused to wear silken clothes due to itchy skin.

Leaving the Home Due to Necessity

- It is compulsory upon the divorcee or widow to complete the ʿIddah in the same home which was her permanent residence at the time of divorce or her husband's demise. However, if does not have enough money to pay basic needs, shelter and food, she will be excused to leave the house during daytime to work. She should ensure that she adheres to the laws of Ḥijāb and spends the nights at her house. It is also imperative that, during the day, she returns home immediately upon being free from her work. Spending any time outside the house over and above that which is necessary is not permissible. If her employment takes up some part of the night as well, she will be excused, but she should spend the major part of the night at her own home.

- A woman who owns a cultivated land, farm, property or business which requires her personal attention and management and there is no family member available to assist her, she will be excused to leave the house.

If such a place is equivalent to the distance of Safar (88 km or more), then she may travel there with her Maḥram (person with whom marriage is permanently unlawful).

- If a woman observing the ʿIddah of Death is ill and it is not possible to arrange for a house-call by a physician, or if there arises an emergency for her admission to a hospital, it will be permissible to take her to a hospital or another city if there is a need.

Shifting Residence During ʿIddah Under Compelling Circumstances

RULES:

A woman may move to another home in order to complete the ʿIddah in the following situations:

1. If the house was rented and she does not have the means to pay the rent.

2. If her share of the house which she had inherited from her husband is insufficient for her to live in and the other inheritors do not allow her to use their share.

3. If she cannot observe Pardah in the home.

4. Any such situation in which her life, wealth or chastity are not safe.

5. If the house in which she is observing ʿIddah collapses, or there be the danger that it will.

6. If there is a strong apprehension that she is likely to lose her honour, life, property or health if she stays there.

7. If she fears living alone and she does not have a trustworthy person to live with her. If the fear is not severe, then it will not be permissible to move out of the house.

8. Similarly, if the house in which she is passing her ʿIddah be haunted and she has a strong fear of demons, so much so that she cannot bear the very thought

of living in a haunted house, or there is some open evidence of harm caused by such evil presence.

In a situation where shifting from the house of ʿIddah is permissible, it is necessary the woman shift to the closest possible house where her life, wealth and chastity are safe. Unless necessary, she should not move to a more distant house. She should pass the remaining days of her ʿIddah in the house to which she shifted.

A Woman on Journey at the Time of Her Husband's Demise

Different situations have different rulings, the details of which follow:

I.   If a woman receives the news of her husband's death, whilst she is on Safar and was within 88 km from her hometown, she should immediately return home and complete her ʿIddah there, irrespective of how far her destination is. This applies whether or not she has a Maḥram with her.

II.   II. If she had already covered 88km, then

    A.   If her destination is within 88 km, she may continue her Safar and upon reaching the destination, she should complete her ʿIddah there, whether or not she has a Maḥram with her.

    B. If her destination is more than 88 km away and

        1. if the place is uninhabited she has the choice of either returning to her hometown or continuing her journey to her

destination and complete her ʿIddah there. It is advisable for her to return to her hometown.

2. if it is an inhabited place where she could stay, she should remain there.

If in case no. II.B.1, en route to her hometown or her destination, she passes by such an inhabited town where she could stay and her life, wealth and modesty are safe, she should stay there and complete her ʿIddah.

Negligence of ʿIddah

Many widows and divorced women do not observe the laws of ʿIddah. Going out openly, visiting Bazaars and attending social functions are activities undertaken in absolute disregard to this injunction of the Shariah. That is a major sin.

Leaving the House Without a Sharʿī Reason

The excuses under which going out of the house during ʿIddah are permissible have been listed earlier on. If a situation of a different nature arises under which going out of the house appears to be necessary, the situation should be discussed with a trustworthy ʿĀlim in order to ascertain the Shar'ī validity of the excuse.

Many women observing ʿIddah leave the house on flimsy excuses, such as to show up at a meeting, ceremony, function, etc.

Going Out in ʿIddah Without Valid Excuse Does Not Annul the ʿIddah

Some people assume that the ʿIddah of a widow who comes out of the house without a valid excuse breaks the ʿIddah and it would be necessary for her to commence her ʿIddah again. That is incorrect.

ADVICE FOR BURIAL COMMITTEES

In the past when our community settled in the United Kingdom, the first burials presented many challenges. The burials needed to be carried out in an Islamic way, however there was a lot of legal processes involved which were not necessarily the case in our countries of origin.

Members of our communities then stood up and voluntarily took it upon themselves to understand these procedures, to develop relationships with the relevant organisations and to provide that much needed link in the chain which would enable the burials to take place smoothly according to Islamic Rites. May Allāh ﷾ accept their efforts.

As time moved on and the size of our community increased, local Muslim Burial Committees started to appear to meet the increased demand due to the population growth. The scope of involvement could be from just providing advice, all the way to providing hands on support throughout the entire burial process.

Many people in our community do not even know the amount of work and effort that goes behind arranging burials. And on many occasions, this is all done voluntarily.

Seeing first hand, the good work done by many of the Burial Committees in England, especially Coventry & Gloucester, I would like to mention some of the Best Practices and areas where the Committees can provide a positive contribution.

Community Liaison

The Burial Committee will be primarily responsible for liaising with 3 different groups of people/services as shown below.

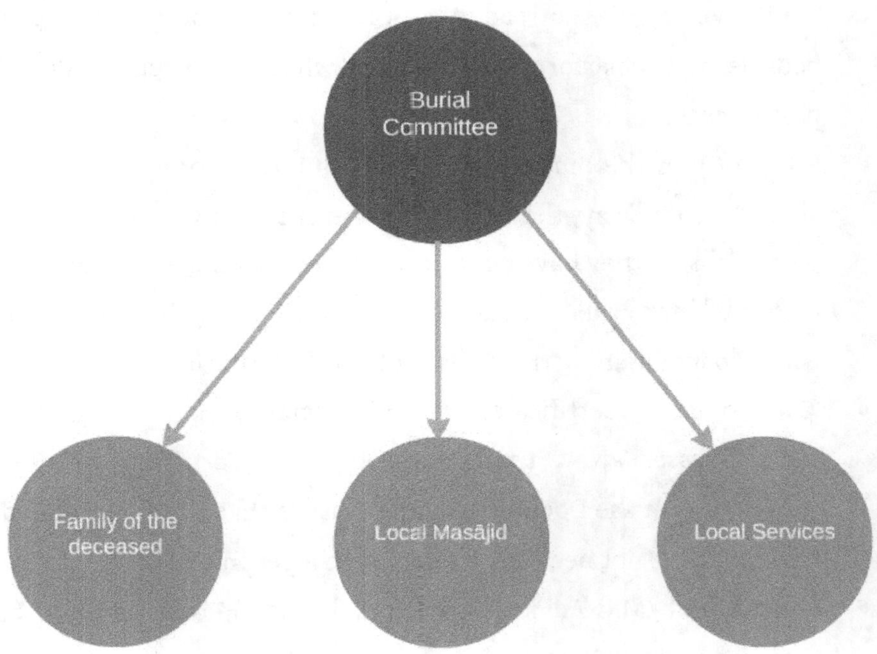

Family of the Deceased

The Burial Committee will be providing help and support to the family of the deceased throughout the entire burial process. This may be even before the person passes away, all the way through the Islamic Rites, the burial and post burial procedures.

Here are some of the areas where advice can be provided to them:

Before Demise

- Put the family in touch with a local Scholar (or Chaplain if the ill person is in a Hospital/Hospice): The final moments are very important, and the Scholar/Chaplain will be able to explain to the family, what Duʿās to read, what Qurʾān should be recited by their bedside, how to perform the Talqīn and what to do when the *Muḥtaḍar* passes away.

- Inform GP: If the Burial Committee is informed of a person who is about to pass away, they should advise the family to contact the ill person's GP if they have not already done so. If the GP has seen them recently before their demise and are aware of the illness, then this will help in obtaining the 'Cause of Death' Certificate.

- 'Cause of Death' Certificate: Advise family, that when the ill person passes away, the 'Cause of Death' Certificate should be obtained from the Doctor/Hospital. Ensure that it has been filled in so that it does not need to be referred to a Coroner.

- Post Mortem/MRI Advice: Advise family that a Post Mortem should try to be avoided. If a Coroner requests a Post Mortem, inquire if there is a non-invasive alternative such as a CT/MRI Scan. If the local Health Authority does not have this provision, there may be some instances where another authority nearby has this facility.

After Demise

- Advice on Legal Procedure for Burial: The family should be informed of what forms are required and where they can be obtained from. Supply them with contact numbers and opening hours of offices as well if needed. Also supply them with information about costs involved.

- Assist in obtaining "Cause of Death' Certificate from the GP/Hospital
- Assist in obtaining 'Certificate of Burial' from the Registrar's office
- Assist in filling in 'Interment Form' & submitting to Bereavement Services.
- Assist in liaising with the Coroner
- Assist in arranging a time for burial
- Transportation: The body of the deceased can be moved from the house/hospital/mortuary to the storage facility provided of choosing.
- Facilitate the bathing of the deceased
- Facilitate the shrouding of the deceased
- Facilitate in storing the body of the deceased until funeral

Local Masājid

Many of the Burial Committees will be based out of local Masājid. It takes a lot of cost, organisation and infrastructure to help facilitate funerals, some of which are below:

- Provision of a cold room/morgue
- Bathing area (normally a raised shallow metal bath)
- Hot Water (Electric Shower with long hose or bucket & container)
- Hoist to assist in moving the body of the deceased
- Metal Caskets for transportation
- Coffins for Burial
- Having a Team ready to assist who are familiar with the various Rites i.e. bathing, shrouding & burial

- Providing an area where visitors can come to pay their respects
- Provide an area to read the Janāzah Ṣalāh if it cannot be read at the Cemetery

Bathing (Ghusl)

The Burial Committee may also have to provide a Scholar (male or female) or someone who is familiar with the rituals of bathing the deceased.

If the Burial Committee is providing facilities to perform the ghusl (bathing) & shrouding, then they must also have the following items in stock at all times.

- Soap
- Towels
- Cotton Wool
- Scissors (to remove clothes, id wrist bands)
- Bandages (in case wounds needs to be covered)
- Shroud (cut to size and also on a roll in case other sizes are needed)
- Strips to tie shroud
- ʿIṭṭar (perfume)
- Camphor
- Plastic Gloves
- Dustbin Bags
- Large opaque sheets to cover the body of the deceased during bathing

Burial

The actual method of burial can be quite varied in different localities. The local Bereavement Services look at many factors before they decide how the burial can take place, i.e. is the ground soft or clay, does the grave require shoring's to support it etc. This will then result in the Bereavement Services making a decision on how the burials can take place, i.e. whether the deceased can be buried within a casket or not. It is always good to lobby the local organizations to ensure the burials can take place as close to Islamic Rites as possible.

Depending on the type of burial, the relevant items must be obtained. Some of which are as follows:

- Large opaque sheet if the deceased is a female, so grave can be covered whilst she is being lowered into it
- Straps if a casket is being used (to lower casket into grave)
- Wooden planks (if casket is not used, to cover the body) or bricks
- Spades and shovels
- Water container (to pour water over the grave)

Local Services

One of the major roles of the Burial Committee is to liaise with the local Services and keep good relations with them to ensure they are familiar with the Islamic burial process.

The Burial Committee should get in touch with the following Services and set up in place arrangements, that the designated persons (from the Committee) will take full responsibility on behalf of the deceased family (after consent) to act and liaise with the relevant necessary legal requirements for burial of a Muslim person in their locality.

Some of these Services are below:

- Registrar's Office: Have agreement where 'Certificate of Burial' can be obtained out of normal working hours if burial is possible
- Bereavement Services/Cemeteries Department: Have agreement where burials can be carried out on weekends and bank holidays
- Local Authority: Ensure the facilities we are provided with are fit for purpose. Also the deaths of any Muslims who have no next of kin should be directed to the burial committee.
- Coroner: Ensure Coroner is aware of Islamic requirements of early burial and the undesirability of Post Mortems
- Hospitals/Hospices: (Wards,/Bereavement Office/Mortuary) Ensure Hospitals/Hospices are aware of Islamic requirements, close to death and after demise. Supply contact information, so if they require assistance, you are there to help
- Doctors/General Practitioner: Inform practices of requirements of early burial, obtaining the 'Cause of Death' Certificate as soon as possible, undesirability of Post Mortems etc.
- Chaplaincy Services: Any local Chaplains who work in Healthcare facilities should also work hand in hand with the Burial Committee
- Police: Act as liaison if Police need assistance.
- Medical Examiner: Ensure they are aware of Islamic requirements of early burial and provide point of contact.

Other Services

There are many other Services which the Burial Committee can provide, tailored to the needs of their local Community. Here are some ideas:

- Parking attendants: Ensure cars are parked properly during funeral and not blocking drives or causing other drivers' obstruction
- Dedicated area in Cemetery where the Janāzah Ṣalāh can be prayed i.e. Leicester has an indoor facility and Gloucester has a dedicated concreted area with lines drawn on floor
- PA System for the Janāzah Ṣalāh if there is a possibility of a large congregation
- Consolidate the costs of the Burial process and maybe have an agreement with the Bereavement Services where payment can be made by the Committee. The Committee will give one invoice to the family of the deceased which will include the costs for the Islamic burial (shroud, transportation etc.) as well as the legal costs for the burial. Once payment is made, the Committee can pay the Bereavement Services for the legal cost.
- Provide Statutory Declarations (Example in Appendix A) to Muslims who would like to ensure their burials take place according to Islāmic Law.

Volunteering

In order to provide an effective service to the community, it is recommended that a dedicated team of volunteers should be available at all times to take responsibility as a voluntary Funeral Director who will liaise with the relevant Services once consent has been given by the families.

It is a hugely rewarding task which will be very stressful at times, as you are always working against the clock. It is one task which will always be required, therefore people need to volunteer to help in whatever capacity they can. Taking away the extra burden and stress from the family of the deceased at this sensitive time will enable them to mourn and attend to more pressing matters

Summary

To summarize, the Burial Committee plays an essential role in the community, enabling the family of the deceased to carry out the Funeral Rites of their deceased with dignity, without stress, in a quick efficient way in accordance with our Sharīʿah.

Burial Committees across the country can learn a lot by liaising with each other and sharing best practices, experiences and resolutions to common issues. It would be very beneficial for each Committee to provide a leaflet detailing the services they can offer and a list of contacts for Services who will need to be contacted once a person passes away.

I pray to Allāh ﷻ that he greatly rewards all the volunteers who work tirelessly, assisting in the bathing, shrouding and burial of the deceased. Who help the families of the deceased and our communities by facilitating the Rites and enabling us to carry out our final Rites according to our Sharīʿah.

ADVICE FOR CHAPLAINS

The responsibilities of a Hospital/Hospice Chaplain covers many different aspects. From supporting and providing counselling and guidance to patients and their families as well as the Hospital staff. It is an unfortunate fact that they will have to get involved in many cases where Muslim patients are about to pass away or have passed away. The family and the Healthcare facility will turn to them for advice and information. Many times, they will be the first point of call for advice on Islamic Funeral Rites.

First and foremost, the Chaplain should make Duʿā for the patient, that Allāh سُبْحَانَهُوَتَعَالَ takes them away in the state of Īmān and makes their journey into the hereafter an easy one without suffering. They should also make Duʿā for families, that Allāh سُبْحَانَهُوَتَعَالَ gives them patience and ease.

The Chaplain should familiarize themselves with all aspects of Funeral Rites within Islām. If they are not a Scholar, it is imperative that they approach a Scholar and learn about the Islamic requirements of the patient and their family during End of Life situation. It would also be beneficial for them to liaise with the local Muslim Funeral Committees so the distribution of responsibilities is clear.

Informing Healthcare Facility of the Requirements of a Muslim Patient

One of the responsibilities of a Chaplain is to inform the Healthcare Facility of the requirements of a Muslim patient who is about to pass away, and the requirements of their family. When special requests are made, the Healthcare Facility will be aware and will not find the requests strange or unusual. The family will also feel at ease. The Chaplain should provide the following information to the Healthcare Facility:

- Expectation of an increased number of visitors if the patient is nearing end of life
- Positioning of the patient prior to demise
- Private room or area where family of the patient can wait, as they may wish to be present at the time of death
- How the Talqīn is performed on the patient
- Islām & Turning off Life Support
- Requirement of early burials
- Preparing the 'Cause of Death' Certificate as soon as possible
- Preparing the body of the deceased for transportation (removal of all catheters, food lines etc. and bandaging open wounds
- Informing local Coroner of Islamic Funeral Rites
- Informing local Coroner of the undesirability of Post Mortems & finding a non-invasive alternative i.e. CT/MRI Scans

Providing Support to the patient and family of the deceased

The more important responsibility is to help the patient and their family. Many of them may not have come across a situation like this before so it has to be treated with the utmost sensitivity. These are some of the tasks which the Chaplain should be able to assist with:

- Location of Prayer room & Wuḍū' facilities

- Supply prayer mats if needed and Qiblah Direction
- Supply copies of Sūrah Yāsīn and the Qur'ān
- Inform them of what Duʿās can be read for the patient
- How to perform the Talqīn
- Advice on Life Support & End of Life Care
- What paperwork will be required, how and who to obtain it from
- Details of Local Funeral Directors so they can arrange for transportation of the deceased
- Counselling
- Act as a liaison between family and Hospital Staff.

There will be so much more than just the above in which the Chaplain gets involved in. Many times, they build up a relationship with the patients and their families. They remain behind after hours and remain on call throughout the night in case they are needed.

Once again this is a very rewarding task. Assisting the family in carrying out the Islamic Rites just before their family member passes away and making them feel that they have done as much as they could have, is invaluable. Many of us cannot even comprehend the emotional highs and lows which the Chaplains go through having to always be the one playing the strong and supportive role. I pray that Allāh سُبْحَانَهُوَتَعَالَى gives them strength and rewards them greatly both in this world and the hereafter.

PREPERATION FOR DEATH

Our whole life is preparation for the hereafter. We have to continuously live our lives in such a way where even after our death there continues to be reward sent forward for us. After we pass away our children and maybe our grandchildren will pray for us and after that there may be no one else to remember us. We must use the advice of the Prophet ﷺ and do those things which he has recommended. The Prophet ﷺ mentions in a Ḥadīth

عَنْ أَبِي هُرَيْرَةَ قَالَ قَالَ رَسُولُ اللَّهِ صَلَّى اللَّهُ عَلَيْهِ وَسَلَّمَ إِنَّ مِمَّا يَلْحَقُ الْمُؤْمِنَ مِنْ عَمَلِهِ وَحَسَنَاتِهِ بَعْدَ مَوْتِهِ عِلْمًا عَلَّمَهُ وَنَشَرَهُ وَوَلَدًا صَالِحًا تَرَكَهُ وَمُصْحَفًا وَرَّثَهُ أَوْ مَسْجِدًا بَنَاهُ أَوْ بَيْتًا لِابْنِ السَّبِيلِ بَنَاهُ أَوْ نَهْرًا أَجْرَاهُ أَوْ صَدَقَةً أَخْرَجَهَا مِنْ مَالِهِ فِي صِحَّتِهِ وَحَيَاتِهِ يَلْحَقُهُ مِنْ بَعْدِ مَوْتِهِ[58]

Abū Hurayrah ؓ narrates that the Prophet ﷺ said "Indeed the good actions and deeds that follow a believer are the knowledge he taught and spread, and the pious son he left, or the Qur'ān he left in his inheritance, or the Masjid he built, or the house that he built for the traveller, or that

---

[58] Sunan Ibn Mājah 238

stream he made flow, or that charity he took out from his wealth when he was healthy in his life, it will follow him after his death"

So you can see from the above there are many steps we can take to increase our reward for the hereafter. We have to look at those which we are capable of and invest in them as soon as possible. It is advisable for the Scholars to ensure they teach the knowledge they learn and spread it far and wide, whether that is in the form of literature, talks or teaching.

All of us are capable of giving our children a good Islamic upbringing, so when they grow up and do good deeds, we will also get a share of them. A simple thing like giving someone a Qur'ān or donating them to Masājid where they will be used is also the source for a lot of reward. Imagine the reward of sponsoring a student to become a Ḥāfiẓ or a Scholar, especially one who is an orphan or from a poor country.

For the wealthy amongst us, let us use our wealth to help in causes which will have double benefit, one for society and the other as reward for us. Building Masjids, donating to good causes, building housing for the poor and destitute, making wells and water supplies in places where water is scarce. There are so many opportunities for us to do good.

The things that we do for ourselves we can also do for our relatives who have passed away as they will not have a chance now. This is known as Īsāl al-Thawāb. Sometimes we have relatives who we hardly knew or were our predecessors, we should even include them. Simple things like reading some Qur'ān and sending them the Thawāb, which is just in the intention, is easy to do. Reading 3 times Sūrah al-Ikhlāṣ gives one the Thawāb of reading a whole Qur'ān, again very simple, not time consuming and extremely rewarding. We should try to do as much for them as we can. If any of our relatives passed away and Ḥajj was compulsory on them i.e. they could have afforded to go, then we should also try and get the Ḥajj Badal done for them.

We just have to think of ways which will attain the greatest amount of reward for the longest possible amount of time and invest in these for both ourselves and our relatives.

I will conclude with a famous Ḥadīth:

أَنَسَ بْنَ مَالِكٍ يَقُولُ قَالَ رَسُولُ اللَّهِ صَلَّى اللَّهُ عَلَيْهِ وَسَلَّمَ يَتْبَعُ الْمَيِّتَ ثَلَاثَةٌ أَهْلُهُ وَمَالُهُ وَعَمَلُهُ فَيَرْجِعُ اثْنَانِ أَهْلُهُ وَمَالُهُ وَيَبْقَى وَاحِدٌ عَمَلُهُ[59]

Anas ibn Mālik ﷺ narrates that The Prophet ﷺ said "Three things follow a person to the grave, his family, his wealth and his deeds, two return, his family and his wealth and one remains, his deeds.".

May Allāh ﷾ give us all the ability to prepare for our death and make us pass away in the state of Īmān.

Amīn

---

[59] Sunan al-Nasā'ī 1911

APPENDIX A – STATUTORY DECLARATION

I

of

Solemnly and sincerely declare as follows:

1. I am a Muslim and following my demise my body **SHALL** be prepared for burial in keeping with Islamic Law that is based upon the Holy Qur'ān and the Sunnah of the Prophet Muḥammad ﷺ.

2. I do not give permission for my body or any of my remains thereof to be subjected for autopsy. Such wish is to be enforced by my next of kin and executors and I understand that my wish shall be subject to legal obligations that would have to be fulfilled.

3. My body or any remains thereof **SHALL NOT be embalmed or cremated.**

4. The preparation of my body is to be performed by Muslims of the same sex **in strict compliance with Islamic Sharīʿah (Law) & practise**.

5. There is to be no viewing of my remains after my body has been prepared for burial and the Janāzah Ṣalāh has been performed.

6. There **SHALL BE NO OTHER** religious service for me other than the Janāzah Ṣalāh and the traditional Islamic Prayer by my graveside.

7. The interment of my body must also meet the Islamic requirement that I (my body) face in the direction of the Holy Kaʿbah in Makkah, Saudi Arabia.

8. Burial shall take place without delay following my death

9. In the event of my death, the next of kin or other Muslim as set out in the schedule below are to be contacted immediately. They shall have complete authority along with any executors that I may appoint to complete all my funeral arrangements that shall be in accordance with Islamic Law and practice.

Schedule

Boxes 1 & 4 can be completed by the local Burial Committee.
Boxes 2 & 3 should be completed by the person.

1.	Enter Details of Local Burial Committee if Applicable:
2.	Next of Kin:
3.	Local Mosque Details:
4.	Other Emergency Telephone Numbers:

I make this solemn declaration conscientiously believing the same to be true and by virtue of the Statutory Declaration Act 1835:

Declared by me: ______ Signed: ______ Date: ______

Witnessed by: ______ Signed: ______ Date: ______

Witnessed by: ______ Signed: ______ Date: ______

Copy 1: Local Burial Committee	Copy 2: Next of Kin	Copy 3: Hospital/Hospice/Care home

APPENDIX B – ISLAMIC WILL TEMPLATE

Last Will and testament of (insert full name)

1. REVOCATION

I REVOKE all my previous Wills and testamentary dispositions.

2. DECLARATION OF FAITH

I bear witness that there is nothing worthy of worship but Allāh, the One, the Merciful, Almighty God, Creator of the Heavens and the Earth and all therein. He is the One God and He has no partner. And I bear witness that the Prophet Muḥammad ﷺ is His servant and His Messenger and the last of all the Prophets, peace be upon them all. I bear witness that Paradise is true, and Hell is true. And I bear witness that the coming of the Day of Judgement is true, there is no doubt about it, and that Allāh, Who is exalted above all deficiency and imperfection, will surely resurrect the dead of all the generations of mankind; first and last and those in between.

This is my counsel to my relatives and friends, my Muslim brothers and sisters, and all those who remain after me: that they strive to be true Muslims and that they submit to their Creator, may He be exalted, and worship Him as He alone is to be worshipped, fear Him and love Him and His Prophet Muḥammad ﷺ with a complete love that is rivalled by nothing besides them. Let them obey Him and hold fast to His Sharīʿah. Let them spread and firmly establish His religion of Islām, and let them die only in a state of complete submission to His will.

I remind them that no man and no woman dies before their time. The exact duration of each life span is precisely determined before we are born, by the All-Powerful Creator, may He be exalted. Death is tragic only for the one who lived out their life in self-deception without submitting to the Creator and preparing for the final return to Him. So, do not preoccupy yourselves with my death, but instead make the proper preparations for your own. Maintain patience and self-composure, as the religion of Islām requires. Islām permits male and female relatives to mourn for up to three days. However, a widow is required to observe mourning for the duration of her ʿiddah (period of waiting). Wailing and excessive lamentation is forbidden by the Creator, may He be exalted.

Finally, I ask all my relatives, friends and all others, whether they choose to believe as I believed or not to honour my beliefs: I ask them to honour my instructions and wishes in this document and not to seek to alter or obstruct it in any way. Rather, let them see that I am buried as I have asked to be buried, and let my assets be divided as I have instructed them to be divided.

Any other bequests you may wish to make can be added here, for example giving up to one third to charity.
I request my trustees to donate to (insert name, address and Charity Registration number): .... To the amount (insert amount) .... absolutely for its general purposes and I direct that the receipt of the Treasurer or other duly authorised officer shall be a sufficient discharge to my Executors. The foregoing shall be taken from my Trust of Residue, such that its total does not exceed one third of said remainder of the value of my total estate. Otherwise, each of the foregoing contributions shall be proportionally reduced to make the total within the "one-third limit".

3. FUNERAL WISHES

I direct my Executors, surviving relatives and friends to ensure that I have a funeral strictly in accordance with Islamic law, which must include ghusl (washing), Janāzah (funeral prayer) and dafn (burial). In particular I do not wish for an autopsy to be performed on my body, and request that my body be released for burial immediately upon death or as soon as is practical. In the event that an autopsy becomes a legal requirement, I would wish that this is met through an MRI scan if my Trustees deem it appropriate. I would also like to be buried in the Muslim Cemetery closest to the place of my death. I am aware that this is a serious obligation and would request that you use your best endeavours to reach agreement over the fundamental matters mentioned and compromise on others if you differ in opinion.

4. GUARDIANSHIP

I APPOINT my (relation) ....

of (insert address) ....

to be the Guardian of any of my children who are under the age of eighteen at the time of my

death but if (he/ she) is unable or unwilling to act for any reason then I appoint:

....

of (insert address) ....

to be the Guardian.

5. APPOINTMENT OF EXECUTORS AND TRUSTEES

I APPOINT ....

of (insert address) ....

and ....

of (insert address) ....

to be the Executors and Trustees of the Will.

6. RESIDUARY ESTATE I GIVE

I GIVE all the residue of my estate (out of which shall be paid my funeral expenses and my debts) and any property over which I have at my death any general power of appointment to my Trustees ON TRUST to sell, call in and convert into money such parts as do not consist of money but with full power to postpone doing so for as long as they see fit without being liable for loss (and such estate and property which currently represents it is referred to in my Will as "the Trust Fund").

7. TRUSTS OF RESIDUE

MY TRUSTEES shall hold the Trust Fund ON TRUST absolutely to be distributed and where relevant invested in accordance with Sharī'ah (Islamic Law), the interpretation and application of which my Trustees in their absolute discretion shall determine provided that such distribution does not breach English Law in which case my Trustees shall apply such modifications as are necessary to comply with English Law.

8. STANDARD PROVISIONS

SUBJECT as below, the standard provisions of the Society of Trust and Estate Practitioners (1st Edition) shall apply with the deletion of paragraph 5 and with the modification of paragraph 6 such that the Trustees have the same additional powers as to the application of capital as they have as to the application of income. NEITHER Section 33 Wills Act 1837 nor Section 11 and 22 Trusts of Land and Appointment of Trustees Act 1996 shall apply to this Will. MY TRUSTEES are requested to have regard to generally accepted Islamic principles of investment and shall not be liable for the consequences of following such principles, nor for any loss to the Trust Fund that may result from investing, or keeping the Trust Fund or any part of it invested, in Islamic investments rather than non-Islamic investments. MY TRUSTEES shall not be obliged to insure any part of the Trust Fund and shall not be liable for the consequences of not insuring any part of the Trust Fund.

SIGNED by me on the (DD/MM/YY)		SIGNED by:	
....		....	
Signature of First Witness		Signature of Second Witness	
Name:		Name:	
Address:		Address:	
Occupation:		Occupation:	

SIGNED by the said (legator) ....

in our presence and then by us in 'his/her' presence

9. APPOINTMENT OF EXECUTORS AND TRUSTEES

Please include Properties (include full postal address), Bank Accounts (include name of holder, name of bank, sort code, account number), Jewellery / Diamonds / Watches etc (include details of where these are stored), Any other valuable assets not mentioned above (please use additional sheets if required)	
Asset 1	Asset 2
Asset 3	Asset 4
Note to Executors / Guardians: When required, please visit www.direct.gov.uk for details on how to obtain a death certificate and probate. Probate is a legal process which authorises the executors to access the wealth of the deceased.	

APPENDIX C -TESTATOR'S FINANCE & ASSET IDENTIFIER

Introduction

This document acts as an addendum to a Signed Islamic Will to ensure that all of a testator's Assets and Financial Dealings are clearly identified to make distribution of his/her estate easier after their demise. Shaykh Yusuf Shabbir has written an excellent article explaining the importance of this exercise which can be found on the following link.

https://islamicportal.co.uk/do-you-know-what-you-own/

Ensure that an Islamic Will is also signed and an instruction placed in it, to refer to this addendum. An Islamic Will Template has been given in Appendix B.

As and when Asset and Financial Information changes, this document should be kept updated. There is a further section in this document which contains information about household bills, direct debits, charity payments etc. which will make it easier for surviving members of the household to handle the finances. There are many instances where this information is only known by a single member of the family and this could cause problems if they passed away without passing this information on.

The information in this document will be extremely sensitive so it is advised that this is kept in a safe and secure location at all times, preferably with the Signed Islamic Will.

Ebrahim Noor 17th Safar 1441 (17th October 2019)

Addendum

This document is an addendum to the Last Will and testament of

Name	
Address	
Date	
Signature	

Assets Owned

Finances – Bank Accounts

List Bank name, account number and sort code. If shared account, list name of partners and state percentage owned:

Bank	Account Number	Sort Code	Partner	% Share Owned

Finances - Money

Enter details of any money which is not in a Bank Account or Investment (Cash at home, cash at other location etc.). If someone else is looking after your money for you, state their name & address.

Amount	Location	In Care of

Finances - Shares

Enter details of any shares which you have purchased, the amount of shares and the Broker through which they were purchased if applicable. If you have any online account details, note them down as well. Also details of any linked Bank Accounts used for the transactions.

Company	Shares	Broker Account Details/Associated Bank Details

Finances – Pensions

Write down details of any contributory pensions you have, associated account details/policy numbers and contact details.

Pension Provider	Account Details/Policy Number	Contact Details

Finances – ISA's, Bonds or Gilts

Write down details of any other type of financial investment, bond or Gilt including value if applicable and relevant details

Investment Type	Account Details/Amount	Provider Details

Finances – Other

If you have any other type of investment, e.g. part share in a company or business then enter all relevant details below: Use additional sheets if needed.

Property

Include addresses of all properties owned, including properties which you rent out to other parties. Details of any outstanding mortgages if applicable. If shared ownership, state name of partner/s & percentage owned by all parties.

Address	Mortgage Details\Account Number (if applicable)	If Shared, name of partner/s, relation, address and % owned by all partners

Other Assets

Include details below of all other Assets which are owned by you including cars, jewellery, precious stones, precious metals (gold, silver etc.), watches, mobile phones, computers, tablets, furniture, utensils, books etc. If shared ownership, also include percentage share. Add on additional sheets if needed.

Money loaned

List details of any money which someone has borrowed off you including repayment details and any dates which have been agreed. Any written agreements should also be kept with this addendum as proof of loan. Include details of Qarḍ Al-Ḥasanah borrowed to Islamic Institutions.

Amount	Details of borrower, name and address & other details (repayment dates etc.)

Assets loaned

List all assets which you have lent to someone else

Asset	Description & Location	Details of borrower, name and address & other details (return dates etc.)

Money borrowed

If you have borrowed any money off anyone, then write this here including the amount, name and address of the lender and any repayment agreements. Any written agreements should also be kept with this addendum as proof of loan.

Amount	Name & Address of Lender	Other Information, repayment dates etc.

Assets borrowed

If you have borrowed any assets off anyone, write them down here including any details.

Asset	Description & Location	Details of lender, name and address & other details (return dates etc.)

Bequests

Up to one third of your total wealth can be given to persons or charities. These parties cannot be your inheritors. If this section has already been covered in your Islamic Will, then it should be left blank.

Name of Person or Charity	Amount	Other Information

Relatives

This section will help any Scholars in correctly calculating the shares of the inheritors from the testator's estate. This is not a comprehensive list of potential inheritors.

At the time of distribution, clarification will be sort, as some people mentioned below could have passed away which in turn could possibly lead to other family members being included in the inheritance of the estate.

Write down the names of the following relatives if they are living.

Spouse

Relative	Name
Husband	

List names of all wives you are currently married to.

Relative	Name	Name	Name
Wives			

If you have recently divorced a wife, and she is still observing her 'Iddah, then list her name as well and make a note of the date of Islamic divorce.

Relative	Name	Date of divorce
Divorced Wife		

Parents

Relative	Name
Father	
Mother	

Grandparents

If either mother or father has passed away and grandparents are still alive, enter their details below.

Relative	Name
Paternal Grandfather	
Paternal Grandmother	
Maternal Grandfather	
Maternal Grandmother	

Children

Enter names of your children, not adopted, fostered or step sons or daughters.

Relative	Names
Sons	
Daughters	

Grand Children

If sons have passed away, enter details of paternal grandchildren (son's sons & daughters)

Relative	Names
Grandsons	
Granddaughters	

Brothers & Sisters

If you have no sons, only daughters, then enter the names of your brothers and sisters.

Relative	Names
Full Brothers	
Full Sisters	

Nephews

If your father has passed away, and you have no children or siblings, then list the names of Full & Paternal Nephews (brother's sons only).

Relative	Names
Full Nephews (Brother shared same mother and father)	
Paternal Nephews (Brother shared same father not mother)	

Household Bills

Enter details of all Bills, Reference Numbers, Cost, Frequency, Account from which they are paid from, or if it a cash payment. Also include any mobile phone contracts.

Address of Property

Description	Company	Customer Reference	Payment Frequency & Date (Annual/Monthly)	Payment Method & Amount	Account Detail (Bank Name, A/C Number Sort Code)
Council Tax					
Water Rates					

Gas & Electricity					
Telephone/ Internet					
Mobile Phone Contract					
Car Insurance					
Mortgage/ House Rent (if applicable)					
Car Breakdown Cover					
Car Road Tax					

Charity Payments & Subscriptions

Write down the names of any regular payments made to any Charities or regular subscriptions and memberships which can be cancelled.

Charity/ Subscription	Customer Reference	Frequency	Payment Method	Account Detail (If applicable)

Other information

If Financial Information is held in a spreadsheet, database or application, write down location and details needed to access file.

APPENDIX D - FIRST & LAST RUKŪᶜ OF SŪRAH AL-BAQARAH

بِسْمِ ٱللَّهِ ٱلرَّحْمَـٰنِ ٱلرَّحِيمِ

الٓمٓ (١) ذَٰلِكَ الْكِتَـٰبُ لَا رَيْبَ ۛ فِيهِ ۛ هُدًى لِّلْمُتَّقِينَ (٢)

ٱلَّذِينَ يُؤْمِنُونَ بِٱلْغَيْبِ وَيُقِيمُونَ ٱلصَّلَوٰةَ وَمِمَّا رَزَقْنَـٰهُمْ يُنفِقُونَ (٣) وَٱلَّذِينَ يُؤْمِنُونَ بِمَآ أُنزِلَ إِلَيْكَ وَمَآ أُنزِلَ مِن قَبْلِكَ وَبِٱلْأَخِرَةِ هُمْ يُوقِنُونَ (٤) أُوْلَـٰٓئِكَ عَلَىٰ هُدًى مِّن رَّبِّهِمْ ۖ وَأُوْلَـٰٓئِكَ هُمُ ٱلْمُفْلِحُونَ (٥)

ءَامَنَ ٱلرَّسُولُ بِمَآ أُنزِلَ إِلَيْهِ مِن رَّبِّهِ وَٱلْمُؤْمِنُونَ ۚ كُلٌّ ءَامَنَ بِٱللَّهِ وَمَلَـٰٓئِكَتِهِ وَكُتُبِهِ وَرُسُلِهِ لَا نُفَرِّقُ بَيْنَ أَحَدٍ مِّن رُّسُلِهِ ۚ وَقَالُواْ سَمِعْنَا وَأَطَعْنَا ۖ غُفْرَانَكَ رَبَّنَا وَإِلَيْكَ ٱلْمَصِيرُ (٢٨٥)

لَا يُكَلِّفُ ٱللَّهُ نَفْسًا إِلَّا وُسْعَهَا ۚ لَهَا مَا كَسَبَتْ وَعَلَيْهَا مَا ٱكْتَسَبَتْ ۗ رَبَّنَا لَا تُؤَاخِذْنَآ إِن نَّسِينَآ أَوْ أَخْطَأْنَا ۚ رَبَّنَا وَلَا تَحْمِلْ عَلَيْنَآ إِصْرًا كَمَا حَمَلْتَهُ و عَلَى ٱلَّذِينَ مِن قَبْلِنَا ۚ رَبَّنَا وَلَا تُحَمِّلْنَا مَا لَا طَاقَةَ لَنَا بِهِ ۖ وَٱعْفُ عَنَّا وَٱغْفِرْ لَنَا وَٱرْحَمْنَآ ۚ أَنتَ مَوْلَىٰنَا فَٱنصُرْنَا عَلَى ٱلْقَوْمِ ٱلْكَـٰفِرِينَ (٢٨٦)

GLOSSARY

Ghusl	Ritual bath
Ḥayḍ	Menstruation
Izār	The bottom part of the shroud which covers the lower part of the body
Janābat	Ritual impurity
Janāzah	Term used to define the deceased or the prayer
Kafan	Shroud
Qarḍ Ḥasanah	Interest free loan given for a good cause
Laḥd	Type of grave (niche)
Lifāfah	The large shroud which covers the whole body
Muḥtaḍar	Person upon whom signs of death are present
Nifās	Post-Natal bleeding
Orhni	The scarf part of a female's shroud
Qamīs	The shirt part of the shroud
Sakarāt	The time when a person is nearing death
Shaq	Type of grave (trench)
Sina'band	Part of a females shroud which covers the chest
Taziyat	Visiting the house of the deceased

www.ingramcontent.com/pod-product-compliance
Lightning Source LLC
Chambersburg PA
CBHW052012150726
47999CB00004B/1631